Emotional Intelligence: An Educator's Guide

"Educating the whole child for life's success means changing the school's curriculum."

By Helen C. Bryant, Ph.D.

Edited by Anthony Ambrogio

Cover Design by Robin Turner

Published by G. Publishing LLC

Printed by Lighting Source, an INGRAM Content Company

Library of Congress Control Number: 2011937628

ISBN: 978-0-9834307-3-5

Charts: The five Components of Emotional Intelligence, and the Emotional Intelligence Domain Associated Competencies included by permission from Harvard Business Review

Dedication

This book is dedicated to all educators of the world who have accepted the awesome responsibility of teaching and who seek to improve the quality of life for all students. May this book be an inspiration of resources to you in facilitating change in the classroom as well as in your personal life.

Acknowledgments

All that we are, as researchers and authors, is a result of someone's assistance.

With appreciation to my Murray Wright High School Colleagues: The late, Dr. Emeral Crosby, Dr. Gabriella Gui, Grady Jones, Linnea Beal Forchetta Scott, Deanna Harris, Cornelius Manuel, Quintessa Washington, Patricia Bryant, and Joan Snead.

I wish to thank my Dissertation Committee: Dr. Elsie Jackson, Chair, Dr. Hinsdale Bernard, Dr. Lena Caesar and Dr. Deborah Gray for the guidance, insight and tremendous support they provided during my Leadership Journey.

To my friends, thank you for the encouragement and for cheering me along the way - Dr. Deborah Spence, Elder Samuel and Helen Flagg, you were there.

Last, but not least, I sincerely wish to express my appreciation to my family. To my daughters, (Sharona & Venitress), my son, (Kyle), my sister (Gloria), my niece (Rosezelle), thank you so very much for your love, support and understanding.

TABLE OF CONTENTS

About the Book

Emotional Intelligence: An Educator's Guide features a study on the Relationship Between Emotional Intelligence and Reading Comprehension in High School Students with Learning Disabilities, and resources that can be used in the classroom. Written for administrators, teachers, and resource professionals, this book is designed for anyone who works with children or who may serve in an administrative capacity.

This book is designed to assist in enhancing or developing an understanding of emotional intelligence and its implications for the classroom, the workplace and church. Additionally, this book is designed to help us gain insight into our own emotions as we strive to make a difference in our own lives as well as others.

Join me as we explore the Relationship Between Emotional Intelligence and Reading Comprehension in High School Students with Learning Disabilities and consider various strategies that can be implemented in the classroom as well outside of the classroom.

Introduction

Despite the heightened interest in emotional intelligence and its relationship to traditional intelligence, the emotional intelligence of students with learning disabilities has not been examined. Although research suggests that students with learning disabilities have social and academic challenges and that these challenges affect life success (Gresham, 1992; Elder, 1997; Berget, 2000; Boudah & Weiss, 2002; Deshler, 2005), studies still fail to address emotional intelligence and reading comprehension in students with learning disabilities. Consequently, because of this gap, and because it is believed that reading is vital to all content areas and that reading affects how students function academically, there is a need for research that addresses the relationship between emotional intelligence and academic achievement in students with learning disabilities.

Organization of the Book

Chapter 1 consists of the introduction and background, theoretical framework, statement of problem, purpose of the study, the research questions, the hypothesis, the significance of the study, definition of terms, limitations of the study, and a description of the organization of the study.

Chapter 2 provides a literature review on the following topics: (a) the historical perspectives of emotional intelligence, (b) components of emotional intelligence and emotional intelligence in schools, (c) special education, (d) students with learning disabilities, (e) challenges students with learning disabilities face, and (f) implications for teaching emotional-intelligence competencies in schools. These are followed by a summary.

Chapter 3 describes the methodology, including discussions of data collection, rationale for quantitative design, population, hypothesis, and instrumentation associated with the design.

Chapter 4 interprets the analysis of the results and the findings of the study.

Chapter 5 provides a summary of the study, a discussion of the results, conclusions, and implications of the findings, and recommendations for further research and practice.

Chapter 6 provides characteristics of an effective Teacher

Chapter 7 provides "educational nuggets."

CHAPTER ONE

Emotional intelligence has become a major topic of interest in scientific circles as well as among the lay public (Zeidner, Richard, & Matthews, 2002). Emotional intelligence is described as having the ability to monitor one's own and others' feelings and emotions, to discriminate among them, and to use this information to guide one's thinking and action (Salovey & Mayer, 1990, p. 186). Emotional intelligence is described as that dimension of intelligence responsible for our ability to manage ourselves, and our relationships with others (Lynn, 2002, p. 2). It is believed that emotional intelligence is a factor that is useful in understanding and predicting one's performance at school and work.

The concept of emotional intelligence might be new to some professionals. However, the idea has been in existence for some time, ever since Howard Gardner's (1983) development of Multiple Intelligence, which included both intrapersonal and interpersonal intelligences (Richburg & Fletcher, 2002). The term emotional intelligence was first introduced by Salovey and Mayer (1990) and was made popular by Daniel Goleman with the 1995 publication of his book, *Emotional Intelligence: Why It Can Matter More Than IQ*.

According to Reuven Bar-On (2005), despite this heightened level of interest in emotional intelligence over the past decade, scholars had been studying this construct for the greater part of the 19th century. In 1872, Charles Darwin published the first known work on the importance of emotional expression for survival and adaptation, a component of emotional-social intelligence (Bar-On, 2005). Meanwhile, educators and policy makers have become increasingly aware of the significance of providing students with educational opportunities that enhance their emotional development (Graczyk, Weissberg, & Payton, 2000). Emotional processes are an important area of focus for students with learning disabilities, specifically in reading (Pellitter, 2006).

It has been reported that the concept of learning disabilities can be traced back 100 years (Hinshelwood, 1917). In 1917, Hinshelwood, an ophthalmologist, reported a case of reading disability in a boy who appeared to function normally in other aspects. In 1937, Orton introduced the concept "twisted symbols," or streposymbolia, which refers to reversed letters. Orton postulated that children with reading disabilities have adequate intelligence (Wong, 1996).

Although Orton is credited for the concept of reversed letters and for the belief that children with reading disabilities have adequate intelligence, Alfred Strauss is credited as being the first to focus on the individual profile of cognitive strengths in children with retardation. Strauss's approach to understanding cognitive strengths and individual differences has a significant impact on learning disabilities because it is the basis for making individualized education plans for students with special needs (Wong, 1996).

Another predecessor in the field of learning disabilities was William Cruishank. He believed that learning disabilities occurred across the entire intelligence spectrum. Cruishank's work was considered significant because its focus facilitated a transfer from the mentally retarded to those students who had normal intelligence but showed distractibility, perceptual problems, and hyperactivity (Hallahan & Kaufman, 1976).

However, Samuel Kirk has been called the father of the field of learning disabilities because of his historical role in organizing the field in 1963 and also for emphasizing language problems (Wong, 1996). It has also been reported that Kirk was the first to attempt to develop a test to measure processing problems in children with learning disabilities (Kirk et al., 1968). This test was called the Illinois Test of Psycholinguistic Abilities (ITPA). Kirk's contribution to the field of learning disabilities also includes techniques for teaching students with learning disabilities. Kirk is also credited with moving the concept of learning disabilities from a medical model to an educational model by focusing attention on the cognitive nature of children's failures to learn to read. According to Wong (1996), Kirk's leadership approach and major contribution to the field of learning disabilities was that he freed children with learning disabilities from labels such as minimal brain dysfunction, a diagnosis which maintains that children's failure to learn to read is the result of having sustained a form of brain damage (Wong, 1996).

Research reveals that, on April 6, 1963, Samuel Kirk informed a group of parents about the term "learning disabilities" and convinced them to use the term to describe development disorders in language, speech, and reading. After receiving this information, the parents agreed and shortly thereafter established the Association for Children with Learning Disabilities (Strydom & du Plessis, 2002). In fact, the ultimate acceptance of the term was due to the political pressure applied by middle-class parents of underachieving youngsters. The parents of these children pressured the federal legislature to recognize underachievement as a handicap caused by neurological dysfunction (Finland, 2004). After organizing, the parents solicited the support needed to legitimize learning disabilities (LD). Congress, as a result, legitimized learning disabilities as a handicap.

Over the past decades, it has been revealed that both researchers and practitioners in the field of specific learning disabilities have disagreed over an appropriate definition as well as the diagnostic criteria. Although there are many definitions of learning disabilities, for the purpose of this study, the educational model of learning disabilities enacted by the Individual Disabilities Education Act (IDEA) was used. IDEA is the nation's special-education law, which was enacted in the 1980s. It provides billions of dollars in federal funding to assist states and local communities in providing educational opportunities for approximately six million students with varying degrees of disabilities who participate in special education.

According to IDEA (2004), the term "learning disabilities" means a disorder in one or more of the basic psychological processes involved in understanding or in using language, spoken or written, which manifests itself in the imperfect ability to listen, think, speak, read, write, spell, or do mathematical calculation. This term includes such conditions as perceptual disabilities, brain injury, minimal brain dysfunction, dyslexia, and developmental aphasia. The term "specific learning disabilities" does not include a learning problem that is primarily the result of visual, hearing, motor disabilities, mental retardation, emotional disturbances, or environmental, cultural, or economic disadvantage.

The concept of "Emotional Intelligence" has been of interest for years. In the field of psychology, the roots of emotional intelligence can be traced back to the beginnings of the intelligence-testing movement when, in 1920, E. L. Thorndike was the first to identify the aspect of emotional intelligence as social intelligence (Goleman, 2001, p. 16). It was then that Thorndike included it in the broad spectrum of capacities that individuals possess.

According to Thorndike (1920), the concept of social intelligence refers to the "ability to understand and manage men, women, boys, and girls and to act wisely in human relations" (p. 228). Goleman asserts that Howard Gardner revitalized the concept of emotional intelligence with his model of multiple intelligences. However, Goleman reports that, in 1988, Reuven Bar-On was the first to assess emotional intelligence. He reports that Bar-On used the term emotional intelligence (EQ) in his doctoral dissertation long before it gained popularity as a name for emotional intelligence and long before Salovey and Mayer published their first model of intelligence (Goleman, 2001).

Payne (1986) defines emotional intelligence as relating creatively to fear and pain. Weissinger (1998) refers to emotional intelligence as the intelligent use of emotions, while Hein (2004) denotes emotional intelligence as the mental ability we are born with. This ability, Hein suggests, gives us our emotional sensitivity and our potential for emotional-learning management skills. These skills enable us to maximize our long-term health, happiness, and survival.

Although the concept of emotional intelligence has been of interest and has been investigated for years, researchers Salovey and Mayer (1990) describe emotional intelligence as the ability to monitor one's own and others' feelings and emotions, to discriminate among them, and to use this information to guide one's thinking and actions (p. 189). They describe emotional intelligence as the ability to perceive emotion, to access and generate emotions so as to assist thought; to understand emotions and emotional knowledge; to reflectively regulate emotions so as to promote emotional and intellectual growth. Moreover, they believe that there are four parts to emotional intelligence, which include (a) perceiving emotions, (b) using emotions to assist thought, (c) understanding emotions, and (d) managing emotions. In order for people to be emotionally intelligent, they must be skilled in all four of these areas (Salovey & Mayer, 1990).

However, in comparison, Goleman (1995) posits that emotional intelligence consists of five components: (a) knowing our emotions (self-awareness), (b) managing them, (c) motivating ourselves, (d) recognizing emotion in others (empathy), and (e) handling relationships. Goleman reports that these five elements of emotional intelligence are crucial abilities for effective living.

According to Bar-On (1997), one's emotional intelligence is an important factor in determining one's ability to succeed in life. Further, emotionally intelligent people are people who are able to recognize and express their emotions. They possess positive self-regard and are able to actualize their potential capacities to lead fairly happy lives. Additionally, emotionally intelligent people are able to understand the way others feel and are capable of making and maintaining mutually satisfying and responsible interpersonal relationships, without becoming dependent on others. These people are generally self-controlled, optimistic, flexible, realistic, and successful in solving problems and coping with stress.

Conceptual Framework

The components of emotional intelligence are reported to include (a) perception of emotions, (b) emotional facilitation of thinking, (c) emotional knowledge, and (d) emotional regulation (Pellitter, 2006). Pellitter posits that these constructs of emotional intelligence affect student academic functioning, and that these constructs of EI provide a framework for gaining an understanding of the emotional processes in students with learning disabilities, specifically in reading. Because they have trouble with reading, children with learning disabilities struggle to learn.

Learning is defined as the acquiring of knowledge or skill (*Webster's New Dictionary*, 2002). Correspondingly, learning is also defined as the gaining of knowledge or skill; the possession of knowledge gained by study; scholarship; or the relatively permanent modification of responses as a result of experience (*World Book Dictionary*, 1979, p. 1192).

Berger (1994, p. 43) asserts that learning is a continual process that involves new events and experiences and that these experiences evoke new behavior patterns, while old, unproductive responses tend to fade away. Behavioral theorists define learning as nothing more than the acquisition of a new behavior. They also believe that the environment shapes behavior and that the changes in a student's behavior occur as a result of learning. This theory relies on observable behavior and is often used by teachers to reward or punish student behavior (Phillips & Soltis, 1998). Behaviorism, as a learning theory, can be traced back to Aristole (Mergel, 1998). The theory of behaviorism concentrates on the study of overt behavior that can be observed and measured (Good & Brophy, 1998).

While behaviorists are concerned with observable behavior, cognitive theorists are concerned with the change in a student's understanding that results from learning (Mergel, 1998). Mergel further maintains that cognitive theorists believe that learning must be meaningful and that schemata structures of cognitive development change via the process of assimilation and accommodation.

Likewise, social-learning theorist Vygotsky advocates that individuals, especially children, imitate modeled behavior from personally observing others, the environment, and the mass media (Isom, 1998). Likewise, social-learning theorist Albert Bandura emphasizes the importance of observing and modeling the behavior, attitudes, and emotional reaction of others (Bandura, 1973). Social-learning theory has been applied extensively to the understanding of aggression (Bandura, 1973) and psychological disorders, particularly in the context of behavior modification (Bandura, 1969). This technique of behavior modeling is widely used in training programs designed to reduce aggressive behavior (Isom, 1998). In fact, rising rates of aggression in schools led Daniel Goleman to study this phenomenon. This research led to the study of emotional intelligence.

Since then, scientists, educators, and philosophers have worked to prove or disprove the importance of emotions. *EQ Today* (2000) further maintains that in the 1950s Abraham Maslow wrote about how people could enhance their emotional, physical, spiritual, and mental strengths.

His work sparked the Human Potential Movement, which could be the greatest celebration of humanism since the Renaissance Period. In the 1970s and 1980s this movement led to the development of many new sciences. Encompassed in these sciences were studies leading to the science of emotional intelligence.

Linda Elder (1997) suggests that, to understand the concept of emotional intelligence, an understanding of the concept of intelligence and emotion is necessary. In standard-English usage, intelligence is understood as the ability to learn or understand from experience, or to respond successfully to new experiences. Elder (1997) refers to emotional intelligence as the ability to acquire and retain knowledge and that its possession implies the use of reason or intellect in solving problems and directing conduct. Elder (1997) also believes emotional intelligence can be perceived as a measure of the degree to which a person successfully or unsuccessfully applies sound judgment and reasoning to situations. Reiff, Hatzes, Bramel, and Gibbon (2001) posit that emotional intelligence refers to the skillfulness with which one can mediate and regulate emotions of oneself and others.

Although emotional intelligence has not traditionally seen the amount of research or exploration that has been given to topics such as cognitive intelligence, mental health, and mental capabilities, studies have shown its relevance to the many aspects of life and the role it plays in the interactions and decisions of everyday life (Harrod & Scheer, 2005). Harrod and Scheer (2005) posit that emotional intelligence is in fact the driving force behind the factors that affect one's personal success and his/her interactions with others.

Emotions are believed to play a significant part in the ways in which we interact with each other. Emotions are also essential in the way in which we perform at work, at home, and at play. Emotions are considered critical ingredients for optimal information processing, social and written communication, motivation, attention, concentration, memory, critical-thinking skills, creativity, behavior, physical health, and our survival (Goleman, 1995; Kusche & Greenberg, 1994).

Emotions influence cognition by providing the energy that drives, organizes, amplifies, and attenuates all thinking and reasoning. Likewise, it is believed that cognition helps us to understand our emotions by providing the words, contexts, and reasons for the emotions one feels (Zambo & Brem, 2004, p. 189). In other words, emotions are the feelings that color our lives and allow us to experience all of the joys and sorrows of life. Emotions are also described as internal feelings which may be negative or positive, and as the underlying force for all thinking (Zambo & Brem, 2004). It is suggested that negative emotions can disrupt thinking and learning, affect motivation, and influence how we perceive and react to life, in turn determining how content and successful we are (Lawson, 2005). Lawson asserts that "when we are happy, we have a clear mind, but when we are upset, we can't think straight." She also maintains that emotions such as joy, contentment, acceptance, trust, and satisfaction can in fact enhance learning.

According to Gorman (1999), research demonstrates that students with learning disabilities experience emotional distress related to their difficulties. Students with learning disabilities tend to have higher levels of emotional concerns, such as depression, anxiety, loneliness, and low self-esteem, than do their peers without learning disabilities. Elias (2004) suggests that these students sit in regular education classes feeling confused about what is being presented and oftentimes have emotions of anger for a variety of reasons (p. 56). Prolonged emotional distress such as anxiety, anger, or depression may decrease a child's ability to attend, learn, or concentrate (Gorman, 1999). Abrams (1986) suggests that constant failure and frustration may lead to strong feelings of inferiority, which in turn may intensify the initial learning deficiency (p. 189).

Meanwhile, Leeper (1948, p. 17) suggests that emotions are primarily motivating forces that arouse, sustain, and direct activity. Isen (1984) purports that emotions influence learning in addition to influencing a range of behaviors such as helping, negotiating, altruism, risk taking, and compliance. According to Robert Greenleaf (2003a), researchers who have also studied emotion extensively have defined emotional intelligence as "the ability to perceive emotions, to access and generate emotions so as to assist thought, to understand emotions and emotional knowledge, and to reflectively regulate emotions so as to promote emotional and intellectual growth" (p. 14).

Pellitter (2006, p. 155) posits that the construct of emotional intelligence provides a framework for understanding emotional processes in students with reading disabilities. In fact, students struggling with reading difficulties must overcome many challenges, including academic failure, poor self-concept, and lack of motivation. In addition to these challenges, students with reading difficulties are vulnerable to emotional as well as conduct disorders (Broder, Dunviant, Smith, & Sutton, 1981; Bursuck, 1989; Grolnick & Ryan, 1990; Pellitter, 2006).

Statement of the Problem

Researchers emphasize that children and youth who demonstrate adequate social-emotional skills are more likely to be successful academically, be accepted by others, be emotionally well adjusted, and enjoy high levels of self-esteem and confidence (Elksnin & Elksnin,

2005). According to Elias (2004), social-emotional skills are essential for academic learning and can improve the school performance of youth with learning disabilities. It is believed that students who receive an education in academics only, an education that does not address emotional-intelligence skills, may be ill prepared for future challenges of the 21st century, both as individuals and as members of society (Katyal & Awasthi, 2005, p. 153).

When evaluating intelligence, one must also consider emotional intelligence. Intelligence is broader than the narrow cognitive domains measured by traditional intelligence and counts for only 20% of life success (Gardner, 1995). Studies show that students with learning disabilities have average or above-average cognitive intelligence. Yet these students demonstrate a wide range of negative traits, including academic weaknesses and social and behavioral challenges (Boudah & Weiss, 2002). There has to be a reason why students with learning disabilities are not successful academically. Empirical studies suggest that emotional intelligence is a predictor of one's success (Goleman, 1995). Although students with learning disabilities are tested for "intelligence," research does not show that their emotional intelligence has been tested.

Studies show that students with learning disabilities who read poorly suffer from problems that go far beyond academic achievement (Gaskins,

1984; Hallahan & Kauffman, 1997). Studies are available on the implementation of emotional intelligence and the correlation between emotional intelligence and behavior, emotional intelligence and extra music skills, and emotional intelligence and academic achievement in college students (McClung, A.C. 2000; Reiff, H., Hatzes, N., Barmel, M.H. & Gibson, T. 2001; Abi, Samura, N. 2000; Stone-McCowan, K & McCormick, A.H. 1999; Handwerk, M., & Marchall, R.M. 1998). However, little or no research is available that addresses emotional intelligence and how it affects the reading comprehension of students with learning disabilities. Thus, there is a gap in the research between emotional intelligence and its effect on reading comprehension in high-school students with learning disabilities.

Because students with learning disabilities possess academic weaknesses and social deficiencies that interfere with achievement, further research is needed. Because of this gap, and because reading is significant to all academic achievement and all content areas, such as social studies, science, language arts, and math, it is essential to explore the relationship between emotional intelligence and reading comprehension in students with learning disabilities.

Purpose of This Study

The purpose of this study was to explore the relationship between emotional intelligence and reading comprehension and the effect of gender and grade level on high-school students with learning disabilities at Dillard High School in Southeastern Michigan.

Research Questions

The following five questions were investigated:

1. What is the relationship between emotional intelligence and reading comprehension of students with learning disabilities at Dillard High School?

2. What is the relationship between emotional intelligence and gender of students with learning disabilities at Dillard High School?

3. What is the relationship between emotional intelligence and grade level of students with learning disabilities at Dillard High School?

4. What is the relationship between reading comprehension and gender of students with learning disabilities at Dillard High School?

5. What is the relationship between reading comprehension and grade level of students with learning disabilities at Dillard High School?

Setting Description

Dillard High School is a secondary school located in Southeastern Michigan. Dillard High School has approximately 1,500 students of diverse background and incomes. Of this enrollment, 95% are African-American. Ten percent of the student body consists of special-education students. Of that special-education population, 75% have been diagnosed as Learning Disabled. The staff at Dillard High School consists of 33 male teachers and 52 female teachers. The ethnic makeup of the staff is 85% African-American.

The mission of Dillard High School is to develop a student-centered, data-driven learning environment where all students emerge as life-long learners ready to fulfill the requirements of the workforce and higher education. At Dillard High School, all students are given an opportunity to reach their optimal level of academic achievement. In an effort to raise student achievement and instructional strategies, the staff is engaged in various professional initiatives. Special Education students are mainstreamed into the general-education curriculum and are able to participate in all aspects of the general-education curriculum and extracurricular activities.

Significance of Study

Goleman (1995) reports that IQ alone is no longer the measure for success. He also reports that emotional intelligence is needed if one is to meet success in the workplace and, further, that IQ counts for 20% of that success, while emotional and social intelligence and luck account for the rest. According to Goleman, we can teach and improve in children crucial emotional competencies, but we cannot teach IQ. In fact, teaching emotional social skills in school is important; teaching these skills has a long-term effect on achievement (Elias et al., 1991).

It is hoped that the results of this study will (a) add to the body of literature on students with learning disabilities; (b) make teachers of students with learning disabilities aware of the social-emotional skills that these students have and need in order to be successful; (c) provide insight as to how educators can incorporate emotional-intelligence instructional strategies into the curriculum; (d) provide other support personnel, such as school social workers, teacher consultants, and counselors, with an awareness of the social-emotional skills students with learning disabilities have and need to meet success; and (e) provide an awareness to administrators of the need to integrate emotional-intelligence skills into the general curriculum.

The results of this study will provide insight for school leadership. The study will be of particular interest to educators and school administrators as decisions are made for the inclusion of special-education students into general-education classrooms and as administrators address student-behavior concerns. In order for students to receive the full benefit of emotional-intelligence training, school leadership support is essential.

Leadership is a process of giving purpose (meaningful direction) to collective effort and causing willing effort to be expended to achieve purpose (Jacobs & Jacquies, 1990, p. 281). Leadership is the ability to step outside the culture, to start evolutionary change processes that are more adaptive (Schein, 1992, p. 2). Leadership is about articulating visions, embodying values, and creating the environment within which things can be accomplished (Richards & Engle, 1986, p. 206). School leaders must learn to overcome barriers and cope with the chaos that naturally exists during the complex process of change (Fullan & Miles, 1992).

In *The New Meaning of Educational Change*, Fullan (1991) describes change as multidimensional. He notes that change can occur at many levels, such as the classroom, school, district, or state. According to Fullan (1991), changes such as new materials, new practices and behaviors, and new beliefs and understandings can occur at any level of an organization. The top management team usually guides major change in an organization. However, any member of the organization can initiate change or contribute to its success (Yukl, 1998). Successful school change rests largely on the facilitators who accept the role of change agent. Rust and Freidus (2001) define a change agent as an individual who fulfills the following critical roles during the process of change: negotiator, nurturer, teacher, learner, and curriculum developer. Meanwhile, Fullan (1991) defines a change agent as a leader who is self-confident about the nature of the change process. Change agents who wish to move successfully from initiation to implementation must carefully consider the local dynamics when deciding how to go about initiating change (Fullan, 2001). He also suggests that, before attempting to change at the local level, change agents must develop an understanding of the psychological dynamics and interactions between individuals in the local community.

The school setting is arguably one of the most important contexts for learning emotional skills and competencies (Mayer & Salovey, 1997). And introducing emotional intelligence in schools would certainly be a change. Teaching emotional intelligence in schools challenges the current paradigm of school-based learning. Educators and psychologists understand that children's emotional learning should be given serious consideration and promoted in schools (Elias et al., 1997). Additionally, they believe social and emotional education is the missing piece of the mission of schools and that this missing piece, although dear to the hearts of teachers, somehow eludes them.

Definition of Terms

As used in this study, the following terms are defined thus:

Academic Achievement: Refers to how well the child is performing in core skill areas such as reading, mathematics, and writing. Assessment batteries typically include an individual measure of academic achievement, although it is important to realize that standardized achievement tests may be inappropriate for use with immigrant or minority-group children. Information about the specific skills the child possesses is important both for the planning and evaluation of instruction.

Achievement: *Webster's New Dictionary* (2002) defines achievement as the quality and quantity of a student's work, and says that it encompasses student ability and performance. It is multidimensional and is intricately related to human growth, which is the basis for emotional intelligence (Goleman, 1995).

Adaptability Dimension: This consists of three related abilities: (a) reality testing, (b) flexibility, and (c) problem solving.

Differential Diagnosis: The determination that a student has a learning disability. Since students with learning disabilities have average

36

to above-average intelligence, schools may not use any single measure or assessment as the sole criterion for determining whether a student has a disability. A determination must include a finding that the student does not achieve commensurate with his age in one or more of the following areas: oral expression, listening comprehension, written expression, basic reading skill, reading-fluency skills (not previously included), reading comprehension, mathematics calculation, mathematics problem solving (previously "mathematics reasoning").

Dyslexia: A specific learning disability involving unusual difficulty in reading. (Berger, 1994).

Emotion: *World Book Dictionary* (1979) defines emotion as a strong feeling of any kind. Hate, fear, excitement, anger, love, joy, and grief are emotions (p. 690).

Emotional Intelligence: Salovey and Mayer (1990) define emotional intelligence as the ability to monitor one's own and others' feelings and emotions, to discriminate among them, and to use this information to guide one's thinking.

Emotional Quotient: An approach to evaluating general intelligence (Bar-On, 1997).

Free Appropriate Public Education: Special-education and related services that are provided at public expense, under public supervision and direction, and without charge.

Individual Disabilities Education Act (IDEA): The nation's special-education law.

Individual Educational Program (IEP): Document prepared by the multidisciplinary team or annual-review team that specifies a student's level of functioning and needs; the instructional goals and objectives for the student and how they will be evaluated; the nature and extent of special education, related services, and the supplementary support and services the student will receive; and the initiation date and duration of services (Friend, 2006).

Interpersonal Dimension: This consists of three related abilities: (a) empathy, (b) social responsibility, and (c) the ability to establish and maintain mutually satisfying relationships that are characterized by emotional closeness.

Intrapersonal Dimension: This consists of five related abilities: (a) emotional self-awareness, (b) assertiveness, (c) self-regard, (d) self-actualization, and (e) independence.

Intelligence: The ability to learn and know; quickness of understanding; intellect; mind (*World Book Dictionary*, 1979).

Learning Disabled: Students who have been formally diagnosed with a learning disability.

Least Restrictive Environment: The instructional setting most like that of non-disabled peers that also meets the educational needs of each student with disabilities (Vaughn, Bos, & Schumm, 2006). The term refers to the IDEA's mandate that children with disabilities be educated, to the maximum extent appropriate, with non-disabled peers. Inclusion contemplates the placement of students with disabilities in the regular classroom with non-disabled students as a right and implies that the right is an absolute.

Literal Reading: The ability to extract information explicitly stated in a reading passage; it represents the most basic or fundamental type of reading ability.

Inferential Reading: Assesses the so-called higher-order comprehension skills and typically requires the student to draw inferences and conclusions based upon material contained in a passage but not explicitly stated.

Word Meaning: The ability to understand the meaning of words as they are used within the context of a particular passage. Such abilities require the student to differentiate among the multiple meanings of words and select the meaning that best fits the context within which a word is used.

Reading Comprehension: Entails understanding and constructing meaning from text and is dependent on active engagement and interpretation by the reader.

Special Education: Specially designed instruction, at no cost to parents, to meet the unique needs of a child with a disability, including instruction conducted in the classroom, in the home, in the hospital, and in institutions and other settings. This also includes instruction in physical education.

Specific Learning Disabilities: A disorder in one or more of the basic psychological processes involved in understanding or in using language, spoken or written, which disorder may manifest itself in the imperfect ability to listen, think, speak, read, write, spell, or do mathematical calculations. The term includes such conditions as perceptual disabilities, brain injury, minimal brain dysfunction, dyslexia, and developmental aphasia. The term "specific learning disabilities" does not include a learning problem that is primarily the result of visual, hearing, or motor disabilities, of mental retardation, of emotional disturbance, or of environmental, cultural, or economic disadvantage.

Stress Management Dimension: Consists of two related abilities: (a) stress tolerance and (b) impulse control.

Delimitations of the Study

The study was conducted using 47 participants who are 10th-, 11th-, and 12th- graders at Dillard High School. Only those students who have been diagnosed with learning disabilities in reading and who met state and federal eligibility guidelines participated in the study. The numbers of students assessed were in direct correspondence to the population of learning-disabled students at the Dillard High School. Only those students who were present on both days in which the data gathering took place participated in the study. The examiner only looked at emotional intelligence, (EQ) and reading comprehension.

Limitations of the Study

Limitations of a study are often not evident until the study is completed. One limitation of the study involved the use of purposive sampling. Because the study was conducted in one school with a sample composed of primarily African-American students, generalizability was limited to other students with similar characteristics. Because of confidentiality, the IEP information was not provided.

CHAPTER TWO

REVIEW OF RELEVANT LITERATURE

Emotional intelligence is thought to play a critical role in determining one's success in life (Goleman, 1995). However, students with learning disabilities present social behavior deficiencies that affect their success (Elder, 1997). This chapter begins with a discussion of the concept of emotional intelligence, and then continues with a discussion of intelligence, human development, learning disabilities, implications for emotional intelligence in schools, and a discussion of successful programs that foster emotional intelligence. The literature review concludes with a brief discussion of the need for educational change.

Emotional Intelligence

Although, many have regarded the concept of emotional intelligence as new, its historical roots are firmly embedded in psychological thought over the past century. Yet the recent rash of attention since the publication of *Emotional Intelligence* (Goleman, 1995) seems to have created a ferment of interest in this way of conceiving human abilities. Emotional Intelligence has become popular in classrooms and boardrooms. Goleman

(1995) proposes that emotional intelligence plays a critical role in determining one's success in life. The question of why some people become successful while others fail despite their natural gifts, abilities, and talents has provoked inquiries into those qualities that determine success (Richburg & Fletcher, 2002).

For years, research has been conducted in the field of emotional intelligence. Studies have covered such areas as identifying methods for measuring emotional intelligence, determining the importance of emotional intelligence skills to one's effectiveness, and applying and integrating emotional intelligence in a variety of settings, including school rooms (Wessinger, 1998, p. 28).

Nada Abi Samura (2000) cites that, in 1968, Cattell and Butcher made an attempt to predict both scholastic achievement and creativity from ability, personality, and motivation. Although Cattell and Butcher succeeded in showing the significance of personality in academic achievement, they were unsuccessful in linking it to motivation (Abi Samura, 2000).

In 1972, Barton, Dielman, and Cattell conducted another study to examine more fully the relative importance of both ability and personality in the prediction of academic achievement. One of the conclusions they reached, according to Abi Samura (2000), was that IQ together with the personality factor—which they called conscientiousness—predicted achievement in all areas. She further states that most of the factors tested are included in the components of emotional intelligence, such as whether a student is "warm-hearted," emotionally stable or unstable, excited or undemonstrative, submissive or dominant, conscientious or not, shy or socially bold, tough minded or tender minded, zestful or reflective, self-assured or apprehensive, group dependant or self-sufficient, uncontrolled or controlled, relaxed or tensed.

In 1985, Dr. Reuven Bar-On developed an approach for evaluating general intelligence. After 17 years of research, Dr. Bar-On developed the Bar-On Emotional Quotient Inventory: Youth Version (Bar-On EQ-i:YV) To his credit, this inventory is the first scientifically developed and validated measure of Emotional Intelligence that reflects an individual's ability to deal with daily challenges and helps predict one's success in life, including professional and personal pursuits (Abraham, 1999). In 1996, Bar-On's EQ-i:YV was the first of its kind to be published by the Multi-Health Systems. Bar-On tests cover intrapersonal, interpersonal and adaptability, stress management, and general mood.

In the scientific literature, the basic components of the concept of emotional intelligence were set forth well over a decade ago (Bar-On, 1988; Gardner, 1983; Salovey & Mayer, 1990), with precursors that

44

extend back to the beginning of the 20th century (Bar-On & Parker, 2000). However, the model of emotional intelligence was first proposed by Peter Salovey and John Mayer (1990).

Although, the basic definition of emotional intelligence is defined in Salovey and Mayer's article on *Emotional Intelligence* (1990, p. 189), another model of emotional intelligence was reported in Reuven Bar-On's doctoral dissertation in 1988. In 1995, the term emotional intelligence entered the mainstream (Goleman, 1995). Goleman reports that IQ contributes only about 20% to success in life and other forces contribute the rest.

In the 1960s, psychologist John Block used the concept "ego resilience" rather than emotional intelligence but noted that the main components of emotional intelligence include emotional self-regulation, adaptive impulse control, a sense of self-efficacy, and social intelligence. Using these main elements to measure emotional intelligence is equivalent to using SAT scores to measure intelligence (Goleman, 1995, p. 135).

Regardless of the different nomenclature used to provide insight into the concept of emotional intelligence, similarities exist in the explanations. According to Byron Stock & Associates (1999), emotional intelligence does not mean being "soft"; rather, it means being intelligent about one's emotions. He believes that emotional intelligence reflects different ways of being "smart." Stock (1999) postulates that emotional intelligence is one's ability to acquire and apply knowledge from his emotions and the emotions of others in order to be more successful and lead a more fulfilling life.

Emotional intelligence refers to the capacity for recognizing one's own feelings and those of others for motivating oneself, and for managing emotions well in our relationships. It describes abilities distinct from, but complementary to, academic intelligence, the purely cognitive capacities measured by IQ. However, achieving high test scores in college is not the factor that determines a good salary, status in one's field, life satisfaction, or happiness with friendship, fame, or romantic relationships (Ekman, 1992). In fact, many people who are book smart but lack emotional intelligence end up working for people who have lower IQ's than they but who excel in emotional-intelligence skills (Goleman, 1998a). Although a comprehensive theory of emotional intelligence was provided by Salovey and Mayer (1990, p. 189), and another pioneering model of emotional intelligence was proposed in the 1980s by Reuven Bar-On (1988), other theorists have proposed variations on the same idea. Goleman has adopted Salovey and Mayer's model into a version for understanding how these talents matter in the work life. Goleman's (1995) adaptation includes the following five basic emotional and social competencies:

1. Self awareness: knowing what we are feeling at the moment, and using those preferences to guide our decision making; having a realistic assessment of our own abilities and a well-grounded sense of self-confidence.

2. Self-regulation: handling our emotions so that they facilitate rather than interfere with the task at hand; being conscientious and delaying gratification to pursue goals; recovering well from emotional distress.

3. Motivation: using our deepest preferences to move and guide us toward our goals, to help us take initiative and strive to improve, and to persevere in the face of setbacks and frustrations.

4. Empathy: sensing what people are feeling, being able to take their perspective, and cultivating rapport and attunement with a broad diversity of people. Empathy also refers to the identification with the state of another person. It is believed that empathy allows us to "climb out of our own skin and into the skin of another" (Licknoma, 1991, p. 31).

5. Social Skills: handling emotions in relationships well and accurately reading social situations and networks; interacting smoothly; using these skills to persuade and lead, negotiate, and settle disputes for cooperation and teamwork.

Wessinger (1998) proposes that emotional intelligence is derived from four basic elements that operate like the building blocks of DNA, and, if nurtured, with experience, these elements enable one to develop specific skills and abilities which are the basis of emotional intelligence. These building blocks are (a) the ability to accurately perceive, appraise, and express emotion; (b) the ability to access or generate feelings on demand when they facilitate understanding of one's self or another person; (c) the ability to understand emotions and the knowledge that derives from them; and (d) the ability to regulate emotions to promote emotional and intellectual growth.

Meanwhile, a revised definition and conceptualization of emotional intelligence has emerged. In Salovey and Mayer's earlier work (1990), they defined emotional intelligence according to the abilities involved in it. One of their first definitions of emotional intelligence was "the ability to monitor one's own and other's feelings and emotions, to discriminate among them, and to use this information to guide one's thinking and action" (p. 186). Salovey and Mayer maintain that this and other earlier definitions now seem vague in places and impoverished in the sense that they talk only about perceiving and regulating emotion, and omit thinking about feelings. As a result of this vagueness, Salovey and Sluyter (1997) provided a revision. The revision is as follows:

> Emotional intelligence involves the ability to perceive accurately, appraise, and express emotion; the ability to access

and/or generate feelings when they facilitate thought; the ability to understand emotion and emotional knowledge; and the ability to regulate emotions to promote emotional and intellectual growth. (p. 10)

This study raises the issue of whether a relationship exists between emotional intelligence and reading comprehension in high-school students with learning disabilities. However, in order to understand emotional intelligence, one needs to understand intelligence.

Intelligence

In 1905, a French psychologist by the name of Alfred Binet, working with a physician-associate, Theodore Simon, developed the Simon Binet Test, designed to measure the intelligence of retarded children. Based upon their observations, they found that, just as children grow taller as they grow older, they become more mentally capable with increasing age. In 1911, the concept of "mental age" was distinguished from "chronological age" (Binet, 2004). Binet, who was largely responsible for the development of the first intelligence test, viewed intelligence as a collection of faculties, including judgment, practical sense, initiative, and the ability to adapt to circumstances (Wallace, Larsen, & Elksnin, 1992). In comparison, Weschsler believed that intelligence was the ability of the person "to act purposefully, to think rationally, and to deal effectively with his environment" (as cited in Wallace, et. al. 1992, p. 105). In comparison, intelligence is the ability of an individual to adapt adequately to relatively new situations in life (Pinter, 1921). Gardner (1986) suggests that intelligence is the ability or skill to solve problems or to fashion products that are valued within one or more cultural settings. Ceci (1994) asserts that intelligence refers to multiple innate abilities, which serve as a range of possibilities. It is also postulated that these abilities develop or fail to develop, or develop and later regress, depending upon motivation and exposure to relevant educational experiences (Gregory, 2000, pp. 139-149). Despite the diverse definitions of intelligence, experts are in agreement that intelligence is having the ability to learn from one's experience and to adapt to one's environment.

Moreover, in 1983, a theory of multiple intelligences was proposed by Dr. Howard Gardner, professor of education at Harvard University. This theory suggested that the traditional notion of intelligence based on intelligence testing was far too limited and should be expanded to include the broad range of human potential in children and adults. This theory included the following intelligences: linguistic intelligence (word smart), logical-mathematical intelligence (number/reasoning smart), spatial intelligence (picture smart), bodily-kinesthetic intelligence (body smart), musical intelligence (music smart); interpersonal intelligence (people smart), intrapersonal intelligence (self smart), and naturalist intelligence (nature smart).

Stages of Human Development

According to Erikson (1950, 1963), there are eight stages of human development. He asserts that these stages, which are referred to as the psychosocial crisis, occur in sequential order from birth to late adulthood. Garrett (1995) refers to a crisis as a person's psychological effort to adapt to the demands of the social environment. Jenkins, Buboltz, Schwartz, and Johnson (2005) assert that Erikson's model of psychosocial development is one of the most notable and comprehensive developmental theories. These eight stages of human development are briefly discussed below.

1. **Trust versus Mistrust:** This involves children up to 2 years of age. In this stage, children attempt to explore their new environment and form basic social relationships. At this stage, babies learn to trust that others will care for them, or they will lack confidence that their needs will be met (Berger, 1994; Garret, 1995).

2. **Autonomy versus Shame:** This stage refers to ages 2 to 3. During this stage, the child struggles to develop some independence from parents while experiencing some doubt (Garrett, 1995). Children learn some self-

sufficiency in activities, including exploring, talking, toileting, or they doubt their own abilities.

3. **Initiative versus Guilt:** This occurs at 4 to 5 years of age. During this stage, children learn to broaden their skills through active play. Erikson (1959) asserts that during this stage, due to the high admiration for their parents, children imitate parents, sometimes overstepping limits set by parents (Berger, 1994, p. 40).

4. **Industry versus Inferiority:** At this crisis, children (6 to puberty) become productive and competent, mastering new skills and obtaining knowledge. If children are unsuccessful during this stage, they will feel inadequate or inferior. Inferiority may occur due to certain failures (Berger, 1994; Garret, 1995; Erikson, 1980). Pickar and Tori (1986) employed the Erickson Self-Report questionnaire and found that adolescents with learning disabilities scored significantly lower on the industry-versus-inferiority stage. It is asserted that adolescents with learning disabilities have difficulty handling adolescence. The results also indicate that these adolescents view themselves as being less capable of adjusting to the demands of society, have a poor self-image, have higher levels of distress and anxiety, and have low chronic depression. Correspondingly, the emotional tendencies would contribute to poor adaptive coping strategies and ego rigidity (McPhail, 1993).

5. **Identify versus Identify Diffusion:** This occurs during adolescence. According to Erikson (1959), teenagers try to determine "Who am I?" It is believed that the goal or theme in life is to determine the purpose of the establishment of one's identity. Adolescents have the need to seek internal and yet external understanding and acceptance (Garrett, 1995). He also asserts that trust, autonomy, initiative, and industry are contributing factors to the adolescent's identity.

Berger (1994, p. 40) suggests that during the adolescent years, teenagers encounter biosocial, cognitive, and emotional changes. The biological changes transform them into adult sizes and shapes. Cognitively, the adolescent is able to hypothesize, fantasize, and speculate more extensively than young children. He suggests that at this stage the adolescent has the ability to understand and create general principles and forms to explain the human experience. Additionally, during this stage the adolescent is able to begin to build systems or theories relative to literature, philosophy, morality, love, and the world at large.

It is suggested that although adolescents have the ability to think logically, their thought patterns are often flawed by adolescent egocentrism, seeing themselves as more central, most significant, and invincible (Berger, 1994; Zenger, 1970). However, relating to parents with new independence, relating to peers with new intimacy, relating to society with new commitments, and understanding oneself may lead to attaining adult status and maturity (Berger, 1994).

6. **Intimacy versus Isolation**: This crisis occurs during young adulthood. During this stage of human development, the young adult seeks to establish nurturing companionship or relationships. If unsuccessful, young adults may experience isolation or loneliness (Berger, 1994; Garrett, 1995).

7. **Generativity versus Self-Absorption**: This crisis involves middle adulthood. Erikson (1959) suggests that, during this stage, there is a need to provide guidance to the next generation by performing meaningful contributions to society by working creatively and raising a family. To be unsuccessful in contributing to society leads to boredom, stagnation, and inactivity.

8. **Integrity versus Despair**: In this crisis older adults try to accept life's limitations or make sense out of their lives. Failure to accept life's limitations leads to despair of goals never achieved or questions never answered (Berger 1994; Garrett, 1995).

Erikson (1950, 1963) contends that a crisis occurs at each of these stages and that each stage requires satisfactory learning before the next stage can be satisfactorily achieved. The identity crisis that refers to the period of adolescence has received much attention in the media as it describes antisocial behavior. Zenger (1970) posits that the adolescence period is a time of distressing inner turmoil and conflict. Most adolescents, most families, and most cultures survive the torrent years of adolescence. However, it is believed that some adolescents with one serious problem may also have several other problems as well. Some of these problems are believed to include failing in school, drug abuse, and lack of close friends (Berger, 1994). Having close friends is important to the adolescent. Zenger (1970) asserts that, emotionally, adolescents are strongly influenced by the desires to belong and to be accepted. According to McPhail (1993), students with learning disabilities continue to face problems long after they complete high school. She asserts that these problems may be manifested in the workplace, in independent living, and in interpersonal relations.

Learning Disabilities

"Learning disabilities" refers to a condition in which a student has a dysfunction in processing information typically found in language-based activities, resulting in interference with learning. Students with learning disabilities have average or above-average intelligence but experience significant problems in learning how to read, write, and/or compute (Friend, 2006).

It is suggested that the history of learning disabilities can be traced back to at least the 1800s (Hinshelwood, 1907). However, the federal government's involvement through task forces, legislation, and funding has only been apparent since the 1960s and 1970s. According to Daniel Hallahan (2000), the history of learning disabilities has been divided into five periods:

1. European Foundation Period (c. 1800 to 1920). This period comprised two main lines of work relevant to the field of learning disabilities, which included discoveries in neurology and the publishing of articles and books on reading disabilities.

2. United States Foundation Period (c. 1920 to 1960). During this period, United States researchers focused on language, reading disabilities, and perceptual-motor and attention disabilities.

3. Emergent Period (c. 1960 to 1975). Learning disabilities emerged as a formal category. It was during this period the term was introduced. It was also during this time that the federal government included learning disabilities on its agenda; parents and professionals founded organizations for students with learning disabilities and educational programming.

4. Solidification Period (c. 1975 to 1985). From 1975 to 1985 the field of learning disabilities was stabilized. The field moved toward consensus on its definition and methods of identifying students with learning

disabilities. During this period, considerable applied research took place and in 1975 Congress passed Public Law 94-142, the Education for All Handicapped Children Act. With this law, learning disabilities finally achieved official status as a category eligible for funding for direct services.

5. Turbulent Period (c. 1985 to 2000). This period further solidified the field of learning disabilities. The number of students identified with learning disabilities doubled. Currently, there are more than 2.8 million students identified with LD, which represents over half of all students with disabilities. It is argued that there are reasons for this growth, while other authorities maintain that many students have been misdiagnosed.

On the other hand, Janet Lerner (1976) proposed that the field of learning disabilities can be thought of as having three phases: (a) the foundation phase, (b) the transition phase, and (c) the integration phase. Lerner maintains that, in the field of learning disabilities, one consequence of the modifications and refinements of the working hypothesis since 1947 has been an accompanying change in terminology. Yet educators and teachers have long been aware of children who have difficulty with school subjects or whose school achievement is far below their capability. Thus the pioneering work in the field now called learning disabilities can be traced to the initial investigations in the late 1930s and early 1940s of psychologist Heinz Weiner and his associate, Alfred A. Strauss, a neuropsychiatrist. The field is generally, considered to have been pioneered with the work of Strauss on the brain-injured child, which appeared in 1947. Terms used to identify this child include Straus syndrome, minimal brain dysfunction, central-processing dysfunction, and finally, learning disabilities (Lerner, 1976).

By the 1960s and 1970s, the term learning disabilities gained rapid acceptance. However, in terms of historical influences, according to Lyon and Fletcher (2001), the study of learning disabilities was in response to the need to (a) understand individual differences among the children and adults who displayed specific deficiencies in spoken or written language while maintaining general intellectual function, and (b) to provide service to students who were not being provided services by the general educational system. Lyon (1996) suggests that the influence of advocacy has contributed to a substantial proliferation in the number of students identified with learning disabilities. He further suggests that the simplest explanation for the increasing number of children with learning disabilities and for the difficulty in understanding and defining learning disabilities is that learning disabilities is not a distinct category but an invented one for sociological purposes. In fact, Lyon believes that students with learning disabilities are not necessarily disabled but have learning problems because of poor teaching. Lyon believes that students have learning problems due to the lack of education opportunities or limited educational resources. It is suggested that, because the "learning disabilities" label is not as stigmatizing as the labels "slow learner" or "emotional or behaviorally impaired," parents and teachers are more comfortable with the diagnosis of learning disabilities (Lyon, 1996).

The definition provided by the Individual Disabilities Education Act (2004) submits a general definition of learning disability. The term means a disorder in one or more of the basic psychological processes involved in understanding or in using language, spoken or written, that may manifest itself in an imperfect ability to listen, think, speak, read, write, spell, or to do mathematical calculations, including conditions such as perceptual disabilities, brain injury, minimal brain dysfunction, dyslexia, and developmental aphasia. Disorders not included in this term are learning problems that are primarily the result of visual, hearing, or motor disabilities, or of environmental, cultural, or economic disadvantage.

However, the definition used during most of the 1970s and 80s is as follows:

> Children with specific learning disabilities means those children who have a disorder in one or more of the basic psychological processes involved in understanding or in using language,

spoken or written, which disorder may manifest itself in imperfect ability to listen, think, speak, read, write, spell or do mathematical calculations. Such disorders include such conditions as perceptual disabilities, brain injury, minimal brain dysfunction, dyslexia, and developmental aphasia. Such terms do not include children who have learning problems, which are primarily the result of visual, hearing, or motor disabilities, of mental retardation, of emotional disturbance, or of environmental, cultural, or economic disadvantage. (Office of Special Education, 2000 p. 34)

In comparison, Strydom and du Plessis (2000) refer to learning disabilities as an invisible disability because the existence of a learning disability can only be deduced from the fact that there is a discrepancy between a child's academic achievement and potential. Research reveals that a person with a learning disability has average or above-average intelligence yet performs poorly because of difficulty in one or more of the following areas: listening, speaking, reading, written expression, mathematics, and reasoning (Strydom & du Plessis, 2004).

The term learning disability has long been viewed as vague, even among researchers, because it encompasses a variety of disorders that often overlap (Allen, 2000). Students with learning disabilities constitute more than half of the special-education population. Further, a learning disability is usually designated when a child is not achieving her expected academic potential based on her intelligence quotient (IQ), which is normal or above.

Prevalence of Learning Disabilities

Learning disability has been the fastest-growing category of special education since the federal law was first passed in 1975; today, more students are identified as having specific learning disabilities than any other type of disability, and this type of disability is recognized as a worldwide condition (Gersons-Wolfensberger & Ruijssenaars, 1997).

Approximately 2.8 million school children are diagnosed with learning disabilities, accounting for half of all students receiving special education in United States public schools, or 5% of the total school population. Of these students, 80% have deficiencies in basic reading skills, such as dyslexia, where much research has been focused (Allen, 2000). For the last three decades, the number of students identified as having learning disabilities has increased dramatically. According to the annual data gathered for the 2000-2001 school year as part of the Individual Disabilities Education Act, approximately 2.8 million students between ages 6 and 21 had learning disabilities (United States Department of

Education, 2002). These data represented 50% of all students receiving special-education services, who make up about 5% of the entire school population.

According to Friend (2006), further investigation of the prevalent data suggests that learning disability has become the fastest-growing category of special education since the federal law was passed in 1975. Further exploration of the data also reveals that, although research generally demonstrates that boys and girls have approximately the same overall intelligence, gender is a prevalence issue, with boys being labeled as having learning disabilities at least four times more often than girls. Research suggests that when girls are identified as having a learning disability as a group, the academic deficiency is usually more severe (Lerner, 2003).

Academic Characteristics of Learning Disabilities

The most common characteristic of students with learning disabilities is their struggle with academic achievement. In order for students with learning disabilities to achieve successfully in high school, they must demonstrate skills in reading, spelling, writing, and language. These students' difficulties may occur in reading, spoken language, written language, mathematics, or a combination of these (Vaugh, et. al., 2006).

Adolescents with learning disabilities struggle to respond successfully to the demanding curriculum in core subjects because they lack the skills and strategies necessary to enable them to effectively process the information (Deshler, 2005, p. 122). Despite academic deficiencies, students with learning disabilities demonstrate a profile of academic abilities that reflects both strengths and weaknesses (Mann. Goodman, & Wiederholt, 1978, p. 52).

Research shows that individuals with learning disabilities usually present an uneven profile of abilities. These abilities may demonstrate difficulties with some types of learning but ease with other types of performance (Mather & Gregg, 2006). Students with learning disabilities often are talented in one or more of the following areas: music, art, dance, sports, drama, and mechanical skills (Siegel, 1996, p. 171).

Reading Comprehension

Experts have different viewpoints about reading comprehension. It has been described as the process of obtaining meaning from print. Reading is considered the key to learning. In the past, reading was referred to as a skill rather than a mental process. In fact, reading was regarded as getting the main idea, identifying key details, making inferences, and interpreting meaning. Recently reading comprehension has been redefined. It is now believed that reading comprehension is the ability to construct meaning from a text rather than merely pronouncing words on a page. Although it is believed that no two people will have exactly the same comprehension of a text and because no two individuals will most likely read under the same conditions, four conditions are thought to affect reading: (a) what the reader brings to the reading situation, (b) the characteristics of the written text, (c) the learning context that defines the task and purpose of the reader, and (d) the strategies consciously applied by the reader to obtain meaning (Cook, 1989).

Although reading is considered to be fundamental to learning, Friend (2006) suggests that the most common characteristic of students with learning disabilities is their struggle to achieve academically. Research reveals that most students with learning disabilities experience significant problems in the area of reading (Bryant, Vaughn, Lina-Thompson, Ugel, & Hamff, 2000; Gersten, Fuchs, Williams, & Baker, 2001; Stanovich, 2000; Torgesen, 2000; Vaughn et al., 2006).

Many adolescent students with learning disabilities fail to master basic reading skills. The basic reading process includes perception, parsing (mental references of the situation), lexical acquisition (decoding), and comprehension (attaching meaning to printed information). Difficulty in reading, as well as other language reading disabilities, such as decoding and reading comprehension, has long been recognized as a major characteristic of students with learning disabilities (Van Etten & Van Etten, 1976).

Reading comprehension refers to the ability to understand individual words, phrases and clauses, sentences, paragraphs, and larger units of text (Vaughn, et.al., 2006). Reading comprehension is also described as the process of constructing meaning through dynamic interaction among the reader, the text, and the context of the reading situation ("Pathways to the 21st Century,"2001). This skill is considered the most important academic skill learned in school, and students with learning disabilities typically exhibit substantial deficiencies in reading comprehension, which interferes with academic achievement (Mastropieri & Scruggs, 1997).

To successfully read to learn, students must be able to read with understanding. Students must be able to read with comprehension. According to Van Etten & Van Etten (1976), the components of reading comprehension include the following:

(a) memory—the pupil recalls or recognizes information; (b) translation—the student changes information into a different symbol form or language; (c) interpretation—the pupil discovers relationships between facts, generalization, definitions, values, and skills; (d) application—the student solves lifelike problem requiring identification of the issue and the selection and use of appropriate generalizations and skills; (e) analysis—the student solves a problem through his conscious knowledge of the parts of the communication; (f) synthesis—the student solves a problem that requires original, creative thinking; and (g) evaluation—the student makes a judgment of good or bad, or right or wrong, according to designated standards. (p. 254)

Students who read poorly often have several problems in addition to poor reading that stand in the way of their school achievement (Gaskins, 1984, p. 467). Vaughn et al. (2006, p. 132) suggest that students who struggle to read may encounter difficulty in (a) decoding words, including structural analysis; (b) reading text with adequate speed and accuracy (fluency); (c) understanding the meaning of words; (d) relating content to prior knowledge; (e) applying comprehension strategies; and/or (f) monitoring understanding. Zambo & Brem (2004, p. 95) believe that children who have difficulty reading may form negative self-schemas and come to believe that they are flawed, lazy, and inferior. In comparison, children who meet success in reading are more likely to be happy and recall positive experiences.

This positive or negative self-perception will ultimately influence their mood or frame of mind. Children who are in a down mood will also think of their future in dismal terms and see themselves as losers, focusing on their failures instead of their success. It is believed that mood in turn has a profound influence on cognitive functioning and is considered to be linked to self-efficacy. Self-efficacy is a child's belief in his personal ability (Bandura, 1977). Zambo & Brem (2004) believe that children evaluate their own ability by watching their classmates succeed or fail. Watching their classmates academically succeed while they fail contributes to low self-efficacy and creates a fertile ground for negative memories and self-helplessness.

Social and Emotional Characteristics

Mann et al. (1978) assert that, as students with learning disabilities enter adolescence, non-academic characteristics caused by social demands and pressures that are external to the classroom may also accompany their academic performance. He maintains that students with learning disabilities experience significant problems in social adjustment, social perception, self-concept, and motivation. It is postulated that understanding the social and emotional characteristics of students with learning disabilities is as significant as understanding their cognitive and academic traits. He asserts that these problems hinder success and adjustment in life. Research shows that 75% of students with learning disabilities may have some type of deficiency in the area of social skills and also have lower social status than other students (Kavale & Forness, 1996). On the other hand, some students with learning disabilities are well adjusted and well-liked by their peers and teachers (Greenham, 1999).

Another common social-emotional characteristic of students with learning disabilities is the lack of motivation. Students with learning disabilities have difficulty selectively attending, recognizing, and labeling emotions. As a result, these students may not have the experience appropriate for making judgments regarding recognition of emotion and empathy (Bachara, 1977). Research suggests that students with learning disabilities are oftentimes not motivated to learn. This lack of motivation could be attributed to the fact that they have encountered so many failures; they simply would rather not try again.

It is believed that this learned helplessness (Schunk, 2000) characterizes students with learning disabilities. It has been reported that these students enter a vicious cycle in which negative beliefs reciprocally interact with academic failures (Licht & Kistner, 1986). It is suggested that, as a result of repeated failures and frustrations experienced by students with learning disabilities, lack of effort and lack of persistence are contributing factors to further failures. Eventually, because of repeated failures and frustrations, these students attribute whatever successes they accomplish to luck, an easy task, or to having received the help of a teacher.

Research shows that students with learning disabilities also have difficulty with self-regulation, monitoring, learning, and performance (Vaugh et.al. 2006, p. 46). Self-regulation and facilitation, an emotional-intelligence component that is critical to obtaining goals, refers to self-generated thoughts, feelings, and behaviors. Self-regulated learners are learners who initiate, direct, and sustain their cognitions, learning behaviors, and affects toward attaining particular goals that involve academic success. In contrast, the students with learning disabilities oftentimes show a passive approach to tasks, with little attempt at self-initiated learning or sustained attempts to learn.

In addition to experiencing academic difficulty in core subjects, social-emotional competence and motivation, many of these students are faced with the challenge of behavior. Many students with learning disabilities demonstrate similar aggressive or acting-out behavior problems (Handwerk & Marshall, 1998). However, the difference is the severity of the problems. It is unclear whether the behaviors are part of the learning disability or whether the behaviors are the result of the frustration of failing (Farmer, 2000). Berger (1994) asserts that it is critical that failing students receive assistance before they fall so far behind their peers that their self-esteem is damaged and valuable years are lost.

Diagnosis of Learning Disabilities

One of the most significant steps in assisting students with learning disabilities is to obtain an early and accurate diagnosis. In order for students to receive special-education services to address their learning disabilities, they must meet the federal eligibility guidelines. Before special-education services are rendered, students are provided with both formal and informal assessment. These assessments are for the purpose of providing a complete picture of the student's academic achievement in reading, mathematics, social and emotional skills, and behavior patterns. A student's cognitive ability is usually assessed with an intelligence test, administered by a school psychologist or psychometrist. This type of assessment informs the special-education team about the student's capacity to learn (Friend, 2006, p. 54). The special-education team consists of the parents, special-education teacher, general-education teacher, a school-district representative, an individual who can interpret the results of any evaluation, representatives from outside agencies providing transition services, the student, and other individuals with knowledge or expertise related to the student, and a related service professional if needed.

Formal Assessment

Different assessments are employed to determine whether a student has a disability. According to Individual Disabilities Education Act (2004), school districts are required to determine whether a student has a learning disability by administering norm-referenced tests or criterion-referenced tests. Norm-referenced tests are those in which the student taking the test is being compared to a large number of students, or norm group, such as the Weschsler Intelligence Scale for Children and the Woodcock-Johnson Psychoeducational Battery-II. A criterion-referenced test is designed to determine what you have learned; comparing you to others is not relevant. Examples of criterion-referenced tests to assess for learning disabilities include the Stanford Diagnostic Reading Test (Karlsen & Gardner, 1995) and the Brigance Diagnostic Inventories (Brigance, 1999).

Informal Assessments

Classroom-assessment information, which is considered an informal method of assessment, is another type of data gathered to determine whether a student has a learning disability. Portfolio assessment,

71

observations, and curriculum-based measurements are the informal assessment methods used.

According to Fuchs and Fuchs (1998), curriculum-based measurement is the process of sampling a student's understanding of the classroom curriculum. This process may require a student to read short passages from books in the district's language arts or English curriculum and answer comprehension questions. By comparing the student's performance to a sample of other students in the classroom or districts, a determination can be made about the student's learning progress.

A second type of classroom assessment is the portfolio. A portfolio is a purposeful collection of the student's work that demonstrates the quality and progress of the student's learning. This documentation may include drafts, final versions of writing assignments, and problems solved in mathematics (Friend, 2006).

The third type of classroom assessment is observation. In order for a student to be identified as having a learning disability, the federal law requires that the student be observed in the general-education classroom, or, for young children, in a school-like environment, such as preschool. This process allows the observer to get a general sense of the student's academic and behavioral functioning in the classroom. The observation process allows monitoring of the student's behavior and its frequency among other students in the class (Friend, 2006).

Possible Learning Disabilities Signals

It is postulated that certain signals are characteristic of students with learning disabilities. However, because students with learning disabilities are a heterogeneous group, only certain signals will apply to any one student. According to Vaugh et. al. (2006), the following signals are reported as possible learning disabilities: (a) has trouble understanding and following directions; (b) has a short attention span, is easily distracted; (c) is overactive and impulsive; (d) has difficulty with visual or auditory sequential memory; (e) has difficulty memorizing words or basic math facts; (f) has difficulty allocating time and organizing work; (g) is unmotivated to perform tasks that are difficult; (h) has difficulty segmenting words into sounds and blending sounds; (i) confuses similar letters and words, such as "b" and "d", and "was" and "saw"; (j) listens and speaks well but decodes poorly when reading; (k) has difficulty with tasks that require rapid naming of pictures, words, and numbers; (l) is not efficient or effective in using learning strategies.

Social Warning Signs of Learning Disabilities

Bergert (2000) asserts that students with learning disabilities demonstrate specific social warning signs, depending on their age group. According to Bergert (2000), the social behavior warning signs of students with learning disabilities are as follows:

1. Social Warning Signs in Preschool Children: (a) trouble interacting with others, playing alone; (b) prone to sudden and extreme mood changes; (c) easily frustrated; and (d) hard to manage, has temper tantrums.

2. Social Warning Signs in Elementary School Children: (a) difficulty understanding facial expressions or gestures, (b) difficulty understanding social situations, (c) tendency to misinterpret behavior of peers and/or adults, and (d) apparent lack of "common sense."

3. Social Warning Signs in Secondary School Children: (a) difficulty accepting criticism, (b) difficulty seeking or giving feedback, (c) problems negotiating or advocating for one's self, (d) difficulty resisting peer pressure, and (e) difficulty understanding another person's perspectives.

Bergert (2000) reports that some learning disabilities go undetected until secondary school and that warning signs should occur as a pattern of behaviors, to a significant degree and over time. Research suggests the sooner LD is detected and intervention is begun, the better the chance to avoid school failure and to improve chances for success in life (Bergert, 2000).

Although students with learning disabilities have average or above-average intelligence, they often do not academically achieve at the same level or rate as their peers. Significant academic achievement deficiencies, specifically in reading, writing, language, and math, are most common in students with learning disabilities. Being neglected or rejected by peers, having difficulty academically, or having difficulty staying focused or being able to sit at a desk for a long period of time, in addition to poor academic achievement, can result in low self-perception (Boudah & Weiss, 2002). Although students with learning disabilities present significant academic deficiencies and instructional challenges, with the appropriate intervention and intensity, students with learning disabilities can achieve (Deshler, 2005).

Implications for Emotional Intelligence in Schools

Research shows that, in addition to revealing academic deficiencies, children with learning disabilities also experience social challenges. Some are more poorly accepted; more often rejected, and have poorer social skills than children without learning disabilities (Gresham, 1992). Frengut (2004) reports that students with learning disabilities need to be capable of gaining acceptance into a societal structure that at times can be cruel and rejecting. In addition to experiencing negative social relations with peers, research shows children with learning disabilities have negative relationships with parents and teachers (Holder & Kirkpatrick, 1991, p. 170).

Students come to school with far more social and behavioral problems than students in previous years. Many of these social and behavioral problems may be attributed to difficult home environments, negative influences such as exposure to violence in media presentations, and poor and absent role models (Elias, 2004, p. 253). These negative influences significantly affect academic learning, achievement, performance, and retention. Consequently, because social skills are critical to school success and overall adult competence, social skills instruction needs to become a permanent and explicit part of school curriculum (Deshler, 2005).

Schools that fail to broaden their definition of intelligence to include emotional development will ultimately shortchange students and short-circuit academic achievement. Educators should view emotional development not as another add-on or something to do in between activities or classes; rather, emotional development should be viewed as an opportunity for success in school (Harrington-Lueker, 1997). If schools are to be effective, they must change the way in which they deal with students and develop effective social and emotional competencies (Ormsbee, 2000).

Research reveals that responding to the urgent need to support the healthy development of our nation's youth has channeled the energies of both schools and communities to foster programs that promote and encourage health and social competence (Schwab-Stone, 2004). Research also suggests that students in schools with a strong sense of community are more likely to be academically motivated and to act ethically and altruistically (Schaps, Battistich, and Solomon, 1997). It has been reported that students in schools with a strong sense of community also develop social and emotional competencies. These social and emotional competencies include avoiding problem behaviors, drug use, and violence (Resnick, et al., 1997).

Episodes of school violence have generated a wide range of public attention and solutions to fix problems of violence in the schools. However, Goleman (1995) suggests that equipping the schools with metal detectors is not the answer. He posits that students must develop skills to manage their emotions, resolve conflict non-violently, and respect differences. School programs that teach emotional intelligence can lead to reduced violence and aggression, higher academic achievement and test scores, and improved ability to function in schools and in the workplace (Edutopia, 2004b).

It is argued by Goleman that the elements of emotional intelligence—being aware of our feelings and handling disruptive emotions well, empathizing with how others feel, and being skillful in handling our relationships—are crucial abilities for effective living. Data from around the world suggest that these human abilities may be on the decline in children in modern economies. Goleman proposes that emotional intelligence should be taught in schools (Edutopia, 2001).

Goleman (2000) further submits data which show that helping children gain abilities in self-awareness, in managing distressing emotions, in empathy, and in relationship skills could act as an inoculation against a range of perils: violence and crime, substances abuse, unwanted pregnancies, eating disorders, and depression, to name a few.

Social and Emotional Intelligent Curriculum

When Goleman authored *Emotional Intelligence* in 1995, there were only a few school programs that offered children valuable lessons in emotional intelligence, the ability to manage feelings and relationships. Five years later, hundreds of schools fostering emotional intelligence exist throughout the world (Edutopia, 2001). The following are but a few successful programs that foster social and emotional intelligence.

The Nueva School

The Nueva School in Hillsborough, California, incorporates a life skills class called Self-Science into its curriculum's scope and sequence. Nueva School's focus is to recognize as well as address the emotional aspects of the students for the purpose of enhancing self-awareness, social interaction, and problem-solving skills.

Karen Stone-McCowan (1993), developer of the Self-Science Curriculum and founder of the Neuva School, suggests that it is as important to be emotionally literate as it is to learn math and reading, because learning cannot be isolated from children's feelings.

Development Studies Center

Development Studies Center (DSC) was formed in 1980, with a mission to help children in Grades K-6 to develop intellectually, ethically, and socially. DSC asserts that building a safe and caring community is essential to children's academic, social, and ethical development. DSC also asserts that children who have a sense of belonging and feel connected to their school will ultimately perform better and are less likely to engage in negative behaviors. DSC's goal is to strengthen students' connectedness to school, increase academic achievement, and reduce the use of drugs, violence and delinquency. This organization offers a school-wide approach to a curriculum which includes social, ethical, and emotional learning (Edutopia, 2004a).

Resolving Conflict Creatively Program

The Resolving Conflict Creatively Program (RCCP) is a research based K-12 school program in social and emotional learning whose goal is to ensure that young people develop the social and emotional skills needed to reduce violence and prejudice, form caring relationships, and build healthy lives. RCCP began in 1985 as a collaboration of the New York City Public Schools and Educators for Social Responsibility. The national center for RCCP was established in 1993 in partnership with the school districts to support RCCP dissemination efforts throughout the country. Three of its schools were evaluated by Metis Associates in May of 1998, and the following results were released: (a) 64% of teachers reported less physical violence in the classroom, (b) 75% of teachers reported an increase in student cooperation, (c) 92% of students felt better about themselves, (d) over 90% of parents reported an increase in their own communication and problem-solving skills, (e) the in and out of school suspension rates at the RCCP Middle School decreased significantly while the rates at non-RCCP schools increased during the same period, and (f) the dropout rate at the RCCP school decreased significantly while rates at non-RCCP schools increased during the same period.

The Resolving Conflict Creatively Program (RCCP) has been hailed as an effective program. In fact, Edelman (1996), former President of Children's Fund, asserts that because of this program's effectiveness, the RCCP is a model program that should be taught in every classroom in America. She maintains that, if we are not going to deal with the violence in our communities, our homes, and our nation, the classroom is the place to teach children how to resolve disputes and how to relate to one another appropriately (Lantieri & Patti 1999).

Promoting Alternative Thinking Strategies

Promoting Alternative Thinking Strategies (PATHS) is a comprehensive program for promoting emotional and social competencies and reducing aggression and acting-out behaviors in elementary-school-aged children, while simultaneously enhancing the educational process in the classroom. Educators and counselors use this innovative curriculum for Kindergarten through sixth grade (ages 5-12) as a multiyear prevention model. The PATHS curriculum has been shown to improve protective factors and reduce behavioral risk factors. Evaluations have demonstrated significant improvements for program youth, including those in general education and special-needs settings. Many organizations have recognized PATHS as a model program. Accolades regarding this program's success have come from the Substance Abuse and Mental Health Services, U.S. Department of Health and Human Service; Office of Juvenile Justice and Delinquency Prevention, U.S. Department of Justice; Promising Program; and U.S. Surgeon General's Report on Youth Violence; Safe and Drug-Free Schools Program, U.S. Department of Education; Best Practices in Youth Violence Prevention Program; and Centers for Disease Control and Prevention, U.S. Department of Health and Human Services (Kusche, & Greenberg 1994).

Collaborative for Academic, Social, and Emotional Learning

Daniel Goleman, the researcher and author who popularized the concept of emotional intelligence founded the Collaborative for Academic, Social, and Emotional Learning (CASEL) in 1994. CASEL's first years focused on gathering scientific evidence to demonstrate the benefits of social and emotional learning to students' school success, health, well-being, peer and family relationships, and citizenship. Since its inception, CASEL has included and collaborated with an international network of researchers, who are practitioners in the fields of social and emotional learning, prevention, positive youth development serving character education, and education reform (CASEL, 2004).

Seattle Social Development Project

The Seattle Social Development Project (SSDP) is a universal multidimensional intervention program that decreases juvenile problem behaviors by working with parents, teachers, and children. It incorporates both social control and learning (social) theories and intervenes early in children's development to increase pro-social bonds, strengthen attachment and commitment to schools, and decrease delinquency. Evaluations have demonstrated that the project improves school performance, family relationships, and student involvement in Grades 2, 5, 6, and 11 (Alford 2003).

Yale-New HAVEN Social Competence Promotion Program

The goals of the Yale-New HAVEN Social Competence Promotion Program are to promote personal and social competence in 6th-and 7th-graders. The objective of the program is to enhance personal and interpersonal effectiveness and to prevent the development of maladaptive behavior. Research reveals that children who participated in the Social Competence Program had improved problem-solving skills, improved peer relationships, better impulse control, and improved social behavior (Elias & Weissberg, 1990).

Summary

Because of the controversy surrounding emotional intelligence, questions still remain. Should emotional intelligence skills be taught in school and should children be taught these skills in school? It is believed that children need to be taught emotional and social skills just as they need to be taught other core academic skills. Children watch and model themselves after others. Thus, because they are so impressionable, their exposure to some television programs, cartoons, and video games during the early years should be limited (Pediatric Behavioral Health Resources 2003).

As cited in *Six Ways to Build Character in the Classroom* (2001), teachers may be able to foster emotional intelligence, good relationships, and social responsibility in the classroom by employing the following strategies: (a) teach lessons through heroic stories, (b) hold students accountable for their words and behavior, (c) establish a "buddies program" to build a caring community, (d) emphasize the importance of etiquette and manners, (e) encourage students to serve others, and (f) teach hands-on lessons about the environment. Some may argue that teaching to the emotional lives of students is not the responsibility of education. According to Elder (1997), there are many points of view from which teaching can be approached. As educators, we can look at teaching in the following ways: (a) as thinking through the content we want students to learn, (b) "handling" the intellectual deficiencies students bring to the classroom, (c) teaching through the eyes of administration, or (d) teaching as riddled with problems as a result of political issues. Depending on our viewpoint, we can consider teaching as either fostering or failing to foster the emotional intelligence of students as developing or failing to develop their emotional lives.

Many teachers and parents alike might well insist that such learning is not a quest for schools but rather the responsibility of parents. However, the family is no longer the ideal place for it. In the Western world, the majority of families have shrunk from an extended community to its strict minimum (one or two parents and one or two children) and much less time is spent in family than in school. What is more, parents are not always in a position to cope with or dispense such emotional skills (McCluskey, 2000).

According to Graczyk, Weissberg, Payton, et. al., (2000), educators and policy makers are becoming more aware of the significance of providing students with educational opportunities that enhance their emotional development and social competence. It is their belief that effective efforts to address students' social and emotional needs can promote academic performance and citizenship while decreasing the likelihood of students engaging in maladaptive behavior such as violence, substance use, and early and unprotected sexual activities.

Research supports that school-based programs that promote social and emotional learning can be powerful tools in promoting emotional health. Evidence further suggests that social and emotional learning is critical to a student's education and success in the workplace. Social and emotional learning are also critical in sustaining and maintaining positive, healthy relations with family and friends. In order for teachers and health educators to produce knowledgeable, healthy, nonviolent, thoughtful, and caring individuals, attention must be given to social and emotional learning (Elias & Weissberg, 2000).

While schools may be considered the ideal place to decrease maladaptive behaviors (Consortium on the School-Based Promotion of Social Competence, 1994; Weissberg, Caplan, & Sivo, 1989; Weissberg & Greenberg, 1998), schools can provide and facilitate ample opportunities for students to develop, practice, and receive recognition for emotionally appropriate and socially competent behaviors, both within and beyond the classroom setting. According to McCluskey (2000), teaching emotional intelligence challenges all the basic tenets of the current paradigm of school-based learning; introducing emotions in schools would be a radical change. He further maintains that well-meaning people who have tried to introduce innovations in schools have come up against considerable resistance from teachers, students, and parents alike and that, without their participation; no such far-reaching change is possible. Before people will support radical change, they need to have a vision of a better future that is attractive enough to justify the sacrifices and hardships the change will require (Yukl, 1998, p. 460).

With reference to change, lasting and meaningful change in education is difficult to achieve as a myriad of factors affect a learning community's ability to rise up and move forward in the process of change (Carson & Johnson, 1997). Leading change is one of the most important and difficult leadership responsibilities. For some theorists, it is the essence of leadership, and everything else is secondary. Managing school change and improvement is one of the most complex tasks of school leadership (Fullan, 1993).

CHAPTER THREE

METHODOLOGY

The purpose of this study was to explore the relationship between emotional intelligence and reading comprehension in 10th-, 11th-, and 12th-grade students with learning disabilities in reading comprehension in a school in the Wayne County (Michigan) School District. The relationship between emotional intelligence and reading comprehension as it relates to gender and grade level was also examined. This chapter presents the research design, instrumentation, procedures, sample, and statistical analyses utilized for this study.

Research Design

Quantitative research methods are characterized by objective measurement, deductiveness, generalizability, and usually numerical examination. Based on these considerations, quantitative research at the Dillard High School seemed most appropriate for this study. A combination of correlational and causal-comparative research design was employed for this study because only those 10th-, 11th-, and 12th-grade students who were diagnosed with learning disabilities in reading comprehension participated in the study. Test data were collected, analyzed, and interpreted.

The Pearson Product-Moment Correlation Coefficient *(r)*, the *t*-test, and the one-way Analysis of Variance (ANOVA) were utilized to test the null hypotheses for this study. The Pearson Product-Moment Correlation Coefficient was utilized to determine the strength of the relationship between two variables (Bluman, 1998, p. 474). The *t*-test compares the means between two groups (Bluman, 1998). The ANOVA (Analysis of Variance) is a statistical procedure that compares the means of two or more groups. One-way ANOVA is one of the most useful and adaptable statistical techniques available (Cronk, 1999, p. 62).

Population and Sample

The sample consisted of 47 students (27 boys and 20 girls) from a high school in the Metropolitan Detroit area. Ninety-seven percent of the subjects in this study were African-Americans.

Purposive sampling was used in recruiting the participants. The classroom teachers of students with learning disabilities in reading comprehension provided the names of potential participants who met state and federal eligibility requirements and referred them to participate in the study. All 47 respondents who willingly consented to participate in the study and who obtained parental consent were included in the study. Forty-seven permission forms were distributed to the subjects, and all 47 were returned. Participants consisted of 14 tenth graders, 22 eleventh graders, and 11 twelfth graders. The study posed no risk to participants. Respondents were identified by numbers rather than by name.

Instrumentation

The Bar-On EQ-i:YVS is the first instrument to be published that assesses emotional intelligence in children and adolescents (Bar-On & Parker, 2000). This instrument consists of 30 questions, is user friendly, and takes approximately 10-15 minutes to administer. Although there is no specific time limit for completing the short form, it can be completed in approximately 10 minutes. Respondents with reading difficulties or whose mother tongue is not English may take slightly longer.

Administration of the forms does not require much training. In small groups of under 10 subjects, one administrator and one proctor are sufficient to ensure that all participants answer individually and on the appropriate line (Bar-On & Parker, 2000). Research assistants and teachers may administer the Bar-On Emotional Quotient Inventory. However, the administrator or proctor should be familiar with or given explicit instructions in regard to obtaining informed consent.

This study was conducted with an examiner and a proctor. A State of Michigan Certified school psychologist assisted with the administration of the study. The Bar-On EQi:YVS was administered in small groups: four groups of 10 and one group of 7 students.

The Bar-On (2000) short-scale model comprises four major dimensions:

1. Intrapersonal (self-awareness): the ability to recognize and understand one's feelings; the ability to express feelings, beliefs, and thoughts; the ability to accurately appraise oneself; the ability to realize one's potential capacities; and the ability to be self-directed and self-controlled in one's thinking and actions and to be free of emotional dependency.

2. Interpersonal (empathy). This component consists of three related abilities: (a) empathy, the ability to be aware of and understand and to appreciate the feelings of others; (b) social responsibility, the ability to be a contributing and cooperative member of one's social group; and (c) the ability to establish and maintain mutually satisfying relationships.

3. Adaptability. This dimension consists of three relative abilities: (a) the ability to validate one's emotion; (b) the ability to adjust one's emotion, thoughts, and behaviors to changing conditions; and (c) the ability to identify or define problems as well as to effectively solve them.

4. Stress Management. Two related abilities comprise the dimension of stress management: the ability to withstand adverse events and situations without falling apart and the ability to positively cope with stress (Bar-On & Parker, 2000 p.19).

The means and standard deviations for the normed Bar-On EQi:YVS subscales and total scale are presented in Tables l and 2. Table 1 relates to 13- to 15-year olds (n = 1020 for females, 946 for males). Table 2 relates to 16- to 18-year olds (n = 711 for females, 750 for males).

*Table 1: Means and Standard Deviations for the Normed Bar-On EQi: YV
Short Scales for 13- to 15-Year-Old*

Age Group	Male		Female	
Scales	Mean	SD	Mean	SD
Intrapersonal	14.65	3.79	14.59	3.96
Interpersonal	19.53	2.98	19.56	2.74
Adaptability	17.13	3.39	16.75	3.43
Stress Management	17.14	4.02	16.60	4.09
Total EQ	68.43	9.09	67.50	9.46

*Table 2: Means and Standard Deviations for the Normed Bar-On EQi:YV
Short Scales for 16- to 18-Year-Old*

Age Group	Male		Female	
Scales	Mean	SD	Mean	SD
Intrapersonal	14.28	3.97	15.26	4.16
Interpersonal	19.28	2.86	20.51	2.59
Adaptability	17.14	3.47	16.81	3.36
Stress Management	16.59	4.25	16.95	4.11
Total EQ	67.28	9.18	69.54	8.82

The Bar-On EQ-i:YVS was normed on a large sample of children and
teenagers attending several different elementary, junior high, and high

schools in the United States and Canada. The normative sample for the Bar-On EQ-i:YVS consisted of 9,172 children and adolescents (4,625 males and 4,547 females) who ranged in age from 7 and 18 years. To investigate whether differences existed for age or gender group, a series of two-way ANOVAs (gender by age group) was performed with the Bar-On EQ-i:YVS. Because gender and age appear to have an impact on the Bar-On EQ-i:YVS, results, age, and gender were considered in the norms. A series of gender-by-age-group analyses of covariance (ANCOVA) were conducted with the total normative sample using positive-impression scores as a covariate, and the various EQ-i:YVS scales as the dependent variables.

Internal reliability was measured with Cronbach's alpha, which is an overall summary coefficient that varies between 0.00 (poor reliability) and 1.00 (perfect reliability). The stability of the Bar-On Eq-i:YVS was examined using a test-retest interval of 3 weeks on a sample of 60 children and adolescents (27 males and 33 females). In general, test-retest reliabilities for the various Bar-On EQ-i:YVS scales are excellent. Four types of reliability tests were conducted, including internal consistency with Cronbach's alpha and test-retest reliability, resulting in coefficients ranging from 0.77 to 0.90 for ages 13 to 18 years. A number of statistical analyses were conducted to determine the reliability of the Bar-On scales with males and females in particular age groups and from various ethnic groups. It was found that the Bar-On EQ-i:YVS scales are quite reliable in measuring the constructs they were developed to measure.

Validation results demonstrate that the Bar-On EQ-i:YVS scales identify core features of emotional intelligence in children and adolescents. Case studies illustrate that the Bar-On EQ-i:YVS is suitable for a variety of educational, clinical, and research purposes.

The Wide Range Achievement Test–Expanded (WRAT-E) is designed for Grades K-Adult (ages 4-24) and measures reading comprehension, mathematics, listening comprehension, oral expression, and written language. A measure of nonverbal reasoning is also included. The WRAT-E includes both group administered and individually administered test forms.

The beginning reading section of the WRAT-E measures comprehension of words and sentences and recognition of dictated words. In Grades 2 and above, reading comprehension is assessed using passages with questions that test both literal and inferential reading skills. The passages include textbook-, recreational-, and functional-reading selections.

The Wide Range Achievement–Expanded Group Assessment (Level 5) is available in five levels and is designed for Grades 2 to 12 (ages 2 to

18). Group Forms are administered by the classroom teacher to small groups of students in a classroom setting. Reading Comprehension and Mathematics require approximately 40 minutes each, and Nonverbal Reasoning takes about 30 minutes. Group Assessment Level 5 contains three subtests: Reading Comprehension, Mathematics, and Nonverbal Reasoning. Even though this test included reading comprehension, mathematics, and non-verbal reasoning, only the reading-comprehension portion was administered in this study. The tests consist of multiple-choice items and can be scored easily and quickly. The WRAT-E was standardized during the 1997-1998 school year on a national stratified sample. Norms included age- and grade-based standard scores, percentile ranks, stanines, and grade equivalents.

Group Assessment Level 5 may be used as the first stage in screening a class to determine students in need of in-depth assessment. The WRAT-E assessment is the only test available with group and individual test linkage resulting from having a common norming sample.

The WRAT-E used a sample of 706 parochial students from a large Diocesan District in a major city in the Northeast. These participants ranged in age from 7 to 15 years; they were about equally divided between males and females, and the group contained adequate representation of major racial and ethnic groups. Internal-consistency reliability was examined using coefficient alpha. The Kuder-Richardson Formula 20 (KR-20) reliability coefficient was also used. For the WRAT-E, where responses are scored 1 or 0, KR-20 reliability coefficients were computed for each age and grade group tested in the national standardization program. For reading, the average reliability is 0.89 for both the age and grade group tested. For mathematics, the average reliability is 0.86 for the groups and 0.85 for the age groups tested. These reliability coefficients indicate that the WRAT-E tests are measuring their designated constructs with sufficient consistency, or homogeneity, to yield dependable results.

For the WRAT-E, test-retest reliability was assessed by administering the same level of test twice with an intervening period of 1 month between the first and second test administration.

Procedure

Specific steps were necessary before conducting the study, including (a) obtaining permission from the school's principal and from the Institutional Review Board at Andrews University, (b) getting collaborative support from teachers of students with learning disabilities, (c) obtaining supervisory support from the school psychologist, (d) identifying students with learning disabilities, specifically in reading, by teacher recommendation and participant's IEP, and (e) obtaining parental consent and student consent.

Written formal consent to conduct the study was obtained from the Institutional Review Board of Andrews University, the school's administration, parents, and student participants. Once permission to conduct the study was obtained, students with learning disabilities, specifically in reading comprehension, were recruited. These students were referred by their Learning Disabilities Homeroom teachers. Only those students with learning disabilities who met federal and state guidelines and who were referred in collaboration by their teachers and the examiner participated in the study.

To facilitate internal controls, one examiner and one proctor, in the same room, and on the same day, tested all students. The administration of the Bar-On test consisted of a certified teacher with at least 25 years of teaching and test administration experience, and the proctor had at least 5 years of teaching and test-administration experience. The administration of the Bar-On EQi:YVS was supervised by a certified State of Michigan licensed school psychologist with at least 10 years of experience in administering psychological tests. Participants were provided instructions and an explanation of response choices before the test began.

In an effort to maintain anonymity with the participants and the school, names were not used. A certified teacher with at least 25 years of experience administered the Language Arts tests (WRAT–Expanded Group Test). Specific oral instructions for test administration were followed. The teacher administered the test after giving oral instructions for test taking and providing answers to student questions. All testing was completed on Tuesday and Thursday of the same week. The participants were administered the Emotional Intelligence Test (EQ) on the first test day. The WRAT–Expanded Test was administered on the second test day. Only those students who were present both days took the test. After administering the Emotional Intelligence (EI) and WRAT–Expanded Tests, I collected, analyzed, and interpreted the data.

Research Questions

This study explored the following questions:

1. What is the relationship between emotional intelligence and reading comprehension of students with learning disabilities at Dillard High School?

2. What is the relationship between emotional intelligence and gender of students with learning disabilities at Dillard High School?

3. What is the relationship between emotional intelligence and grade level of students with learning disabilities at Dillard High School?

4. What is the relationship between reading comprehension and gender of students with learning disabilities at Dillard High School?

5. What is the relationship between reading comprehension and grade level of students with learning disabilities at Dillard High School?

Null Hypotheses and Related Statistical Analyses

The data for this study were analyzed using the Statistical Package for Social Sciences (SPSS, 2000). All tests were conducted at a significance level of alpha ($<.05$). The five null hypotheses correspond with research questions 1-5. The null hypotheses were as follows:

Null Hypothesis 1: There is no relationship between emotional intelligence and reading comprehension of students with learning disabilities at Dillard High School. The Pearson-Product Moment Correlation Coefficient is the statistical method used to test this null hypothesis.

Null hypothesis 2: There is no relationship between emotional intelligence and gender of students with learning disabilities at Dillard High School. The *t*-test for independent samples is the statistical method used to test this null hypothesis.

Null hypothesis 3: There is no relationship between emotional intelligence and grade level of students with learning disabilities at Dillard High School. The statistical method used was the one-way ANOVA.

Null hypothesis 4: There is no relationship between reading comprehension and gender of students with learning disabilities at Dillard High School. The *t*-test for independent samples is the statistical method used to test this null hypothesis.

Null hypothesis 5: There is no relationship between academic achievement and grade level of students with learning disabilities at Dillard High School. The statistical method used was the one-way ANOVA.

Summary

This chapter summarized the methodology utilized in this study to explore the relationship between emotional intelligence and reading comprehension in high-school students with learning disabilities at Dillard High School. The sections discussed were research design, population and sample, instrumentation, procedure, research questions, and hypothesis and statistical analysis. Also presented were the criteria for conducting the study. Quantitative research methods were employed in this study. The selections of subjects were also discussed, including the method for recruitment. The population consisted of 10th graders, 11th graders and 12th graders.

The instruments utilized in this study which included the Bar-On Emotional Intelligence Questionnaire (Bar-On EQi:YVS) and the Wide Range Achievement–Expanded (WRAT-E Reading Comprehension Test) were discussed.

This study centered around five research questions, which were presented along with the statistical methods.

CHAPTER FOUR

ANALYSIS OF DATA

The purpose of this study was to explore the relationship between emotional intelligence and reading comprehension in 10th-, 11th-, and 12th-grade students with learning disabilities in a school in the Wayne County (Southeast Michigan) School District. The relationship between emotional intelligence and reading comprehension as it relates to gender and grade level was also examined. This chapter presents the results of the investigation and the statistical analysis of the data, including the demographic characteristics, and the relationship between emotional intelligence, gender, grade level, and reading comprehension.

Description of the Sample

A purposive sample was utilized in recruiting 47 10th-, 11th-, and 12th-grade students with learning disabilities from a high school in the Wayne County School District. Table 3 presents the composition of the sample by gender. As described in Table 3, 20 female (42.6%) and 27 male (57.4%) respondents participated in the study, representing a 100% response rate. There were slightly more males than females.

103

Fourteen 10th- graders (29.8%), 22 11th- graders (46.8%), and 11 12th- graders (23.4%) participated in the study. Table 4 presents the respondents by grade level.

Table 3: Respondents by Gender

Gender	n	%
Female	20	42.6
Male	27	57.4
Total	47	100.0

Table 4: *Respondents by Grade Level*

Grade	n	%
Grade 10	14	29.8
Grade 11	22	46.8
Grade 12	11	23.4
Total	47	100.0

Achievement Tests–Expanded were administered by examiners with 10 to 28 years of test-administration experience. Prior to administering the test, examiners provided instructions and allotted time for the students to ask questions regarding the tests. After the examiners provided the test instructions, they gave a test booklet to each student.

Instrumentation

The Bar-On EQi:YVS (emotional intelligence quotient) and the Wide Range Achievement Test (Reading Comprehension) were administered to explore the relationship between emotional intelligence and academic achievement in high-school students with learning disabilities. The participants were asked to complete the Bar-On EQi:YVS, which consisted of 30 questions that assessed emotional intelligence. The Bar-On EQi:YVS was administered in approximately 30 minutes.

The means and standard deviations for the Bar-On EQi-YVS subscales and total scale found in this study are presented in Table 5.

Table 5: Means and Standard Deviations for the Normed Bar-On EQi: YVS Scales

Scales	n	Mean	Standard Deviation
Intrapersonal	47	14.27	3.26
Interpersonal	47	18.00	3.21
Adaptability	47	16.04	3.45
Stress Management	47	13.31	4.08
Scale Total	47	61.62	14.00

The Wide Range Achievement Test, which consisted of 45 questions, assessed reading comprehension. Certified professionals with 10 to 28 years of test-administration experience administered this instrument as well. Participants' names were not used. The tests were organized and color-coded by grade level. Due to internal constraints, the tests were administered within a 2-day time period. Following the tests, the color-coded data were collected, organized, and analyzed.

Research Questions, Null Hypotheses, and Results

The analysis of this data is organized on the basis of five research questions and their related null hypotheses. In each case, the research question is presented, followed by the null hypothesis and the results of the statistical test.

Research Question 1

What is the relationship between emotional intelligence and reading comprehension in high-school students with learning disabilities at Dillard High School?

Null hypothesis 1: There is no relationship between emotional intelligence and reading comprehension.

The Pearson correlation was utilized in determining the relationship between the total EQ score and reading comprehension. The null hypothesis was rejected. A significant correlation was found ($r = 0.90$, $p = 0.000$), indicating a strong relationship between emotional intelligence (EQ total score) and reading comprehension (WRAT–Expanded). This means that 81% of the variance in reading comprehension can be explained by the variance in emotional intelligence.

The total score for EQ ranged from 55 to 93 with a mean of 76.50. The total scores for reading comprehension ranged from 2.0 to 26.0 with a mean of 11.96. Cronbach's alpha reliability coefficient for the EQ was 0.71.

Research Question 2

What is the relationship between emotional intelligence and gender in high-school students with learning disabilities at Dillard High School?

Null hypothesis 2: There is no relationship between emotional intelligence and gender in high-school students with learning disabilities.

To test this hypothesis, a *t*-test was utilized. The null hypothesis was retained (t = .02, *df* = 45, *p* = .98). The mean for males was 71.66, and the mean for females was 71.60. Therefore, there is no significant relationship between emotional intelligence and gender in high-school students with learning disabilities at Dillard High School.

Research Question 3

What is the relationship between emotional intelligence and grade level of students with learning disabilities at Dillard High School?

Null hypothesis 3: There is no relationship between emotional intelligence and grade level with students with learning disabilities at Dillard High School.

To test this hypothesis, a one-way ANOVA was performed to retain or reject the null hypothesis. The null hypothesis was retained ($F_{2, 44}$, = 0.52,

p = 0.60). Therefore, there is no significant relationship between emotional intelligence total score and grade level. Table 6 presents the results of this statistical procedure.

Table 6: The ANOVA Table of Total EQ Score by Grade Level

	SS	df	MS	F	sig
Between Groups	94.150	2	47.075	0.518	0.599
Within Groups	3998.701	44	90.880		
Total	4092.851	46			

Research Question 4

What is the relationship between reading comprehension and gender of students with learning disabilities at Dillard High School?

Null hypothesis 4: There is no relationship between reading comprehension and gender of students with learning disabilities at Dillard High School.

To test this hypothesis, the t test statistical method was used. The null hypothesis is retained (t = 0.95, df = 45, p = 0.35). Therefore, there is no relationship between reading comprehension and gender of students with learning disabilities at Dillard High.

Research Question 5

What is the relationship between reading comprehension and grade level of students with learning disabilities at Dillard High School?

Null hypothesis 5: There is no relationship between reading comprehension and grade level of students with learning disabilities at Dillard High School?

To test this hypothesis, a one-way ANOVA was utilized to determine if there was a difference based on grade level. The null hypothesis is retained ($F_{2, 44} = 0.84$, $p = 0.44$). Therefore, there is no significant relationship between reading comprehension and grade level. Table 7 presents the relationship between academic achievement and grade level.

Table 7: The ANOVA Table of Reading Comprehension by Grade Level

	SS	df	MS	F	sig
Between Groups	48.415	2	24.207	0.842	0.438
Within Groups	1265.500	44	28.761		
Total	1313.915	46			

Summary and Findings

This chapter dealt with the findings of the relationship between emotional intelligence and reading comprehension in high-school students with learning disabilities at Dillard High School. This chapter presented a breakdown of the sample by grade and gender. Null hypotheses related to emotional intelligence, reading comprehension, gender, and grade level were analyzed. The analysis of these findings was presented on the basis of the research questions and related null hypotheses. Results indicated that there is a significant relationship between emotional intelligence and reading comprehension academic achievement. Gender and grade did not seem to affect emotional intelligence or reading comprehension in high-school students with learning disabilities at Dillard High School.

CHAPTER FIVE

SUMMARY, DISCUSSION, AND CONCLUSION

Introduction

This chapter contains a summary of the study, including the statement of the problem, purpose of the study, and overview of the literature. The chapter also contains the methodology and analysis of the results, followed by a discussion of the results. Conclusions, implications for teaching emotional intelligence competencies in schools, and recommendations for further study are based on the research.

Summary

Statement of the Problem

Despite the heightened interest in emotional intelligence and its relationship to traditional intelligence, the emotional intelligence of students with learning disabilities has not been examined. Although research suggests that students with learning disabilities have social and academic challenges and that these challenges affect life success (Gresham 1992; Elder, 1997; Berget 2000; Boudah & Weiss 2002; & Deshler, 2005), studies still fail to address emotional intelligence and reading comprehension in students with learning disabilities. Consequently, because of this gap, and because it is believed that reading is vital to all content areas and that reading affects a student's academic function, there is a need for research that addresses the relationship between emotional intelligence and academic achievement in students with learning disabilities.

Purpose of the Study

The purpose of the study was to explore the relationship between emotional intelligence and reading comprehension in 10th-, 11th- and 12th-grade students with learning disabilities at a school in Southeastern Michigan. The relationship between emotional intelligence as it relates to gender and grade level was also examined.

Overview of the Literature

In studying this phenomenon, researchers began looking at emotional intelligence and found that emotional intelligence plays a vital part in determining one's success in life. The fact that some people become more successful than others despite one's natural talents, gifts, skills, abilities, or intelligence, has sparked much interest in examining qualities that determine success. Although some people have a variety of natural talents, gifts, abilities, and intelligence, they are not often the most successful, wealthy, or happy (Richburg & Fletcher, 2002).

The concept of emotional intelligence has been around for a number of years. Yet it continues to be an intriguing buzzword in corporations as well as classrooms. Emotional intelligence is "a type of social intelligence that involves the ability to monitor one's own and others' emotions, to discriminate among them and to use this thinking to guide one's thinking and actions" (Salovey & Mayer, 1990, p. 189). According to Salovey & Mayer, emotional intelligence can be broken down into five domains: (a) knowing one's own emotions, (b) managing emotions, (c) motivating oneself, (d) recognizing emotions in others, and (e) handling relationships.

Knowing one's own emotions is the self-awareness stage where one is able to recognize one's own feeling as the emotion takes place. This concept of recognizing one's feelings is considered the "stone" of emotional intelligence (Shapiro, 1998). Learning to identify emotions and being able to convey those emotions is considered to be vital to meeting basic needs. This domain is the key to communication, gaining emotional control, and nurturing relations.

Managing one's own emotions is also essential. Goleman (1995) posits that, when enduring life's positive and negative challenges, having the ability to handle feelings appropriately, with a degree of balance, has an influence on our emotional well being and stability. Emotional control refers to the ability to keep calm and retain a high level of performance under stress and to deal with stress or conflict in the social environment. Cherness and Adler, (2000) report that having the ability to perceive, identify and manage emotions provides the basis for social-emotional competencies that are critical for success in almost any employment.

Motivating oneself can be considered the degree to which an individual acts upon a given thought, idea, or goal (Richburg & Fletcher, 2002, p. 33). Motivating oneself can be viewed as a state of mind in which the individual examines factors such as desire, gratification, outcome, benefits, or sacrifices that a behavior is directed toward achieving rather than the behavior itself (Zirker, 2000, p. 5).

Recognizing the emotional state of others and being sensitive to emotions (empathy) is viewed as interpersonal intelligence. This ability allows one to discriminate and recognize or detect moods and feelings of other individuals (Gardner, 1983, p. 239). It is believed that this skill of being sensitive to others molds our social competence and contributes to occupational success. How one relates to others is a vital social-competence skill. Goleman posits that, "emotions are contagious" (1995, p. 114).

The fifth domain, handling relationships, includes maintaining relationships with all types of people. This skill is also vital because it is influenced by all other components of emotional intelligence (Richburg & Fletcher, 2002, p. 36).

In order to understand the concept of emotional intelligence, one must understand intelligence. Wallace et. al. (1992) posit that intelligence can be viewed as a collection of faculties, involving judgment, practical sense, initiative, and the ability to adapt to circumstances. Intelligence can also be perceived as the ability to act purposefully, to think rationally, and to deal effectively with one's environment.

Students with learning disabilities exhibit average to above-average intelligence. However, students with learning disabilities also demonstrate deficiencies in reading, writing, language, and math, and often they do not achieve at the same rate as their peers. The term "learning disabilities" has also generated controversy for years; historically, its origin can be traced back to at the least the 1800s.

There are different definitions for the term *learning disabilities*. However, for this study, the educational model is used. After three years of debate and compromise, America's federal law governing special education has been revised. Here is the revised definition for learning disabilities, according to the Individuals Disabilities Education Act (IDEA):

> A 'specific learning disability' [is] a disorder as in one or more of the basic psychological processes involved in understanding or in using language, spoken or written, which disorder may manifest itself in the imperfect ability to listen, think, speak, read, write, spell, or do mathematical calculations. (Individual Disabilities Education Act, 2004)

Specific learning disabilities include conditions as perceptual disabilities, brain injury, minimal brain dysfunction, dyslexia, and developmental aphasia. However, specific learning disabilities do not include a learning problem that is primarily the result of visual, hearing, or motor disabilities, of mental retardation, of emotional disturbance, or of environmental, cultural, or economic disadvantage.

IDEA's 2004 revisions contain provisions that aim to strengthen how special-education students are diagnosed and academic progress is measured. The revised rule was enacted to ensure that all special-needs students are given access to high-quality instruction in reading and math as well as sufficient time and instruction to acquire English-language skills before being determined to have a disability. A student should not be determined to have a specific learning disability if the learning problems are due to the student's lack of appropriate instruction in math, reading (including phonemic awareness, phonics, vocabulary development, reading fluency), or reading-comprehension strategies or because the student has limited English proficiency (Baumel, 2003).

According to IDEA, schools may not use any single measure or assessment as the sole criterion for determining whether a student has a disability. When identifying specific learning disabilities, more assessments such as those that evaluate a student's information-processing abilities, intellectual capacity, and overall health are required. The multidisciplinary team that evaluates the student must also determine that the student's academic difficulties are not primarily caused by other factors or due to lack of high-quality instruction. This requirement is prescribed by the federal No Child Left Behind Act (NCLB).

Before the revisions, the process used in determining specific–learning-disability eligibility was known as the discrepancy model. The model measures the discrepancy between a child's academic achievement or academic performance and his intellectual ability. If there was a significant difference in the child's intellectual score or cognitive score and his performance score, it was then determined that the student had a learning disability. It is believed that, by using this model, the student could receive services that would improve his or her performance level.

Critics called the discrepancy model the "wait-to-fail" model because it required a child to academically fall behind his or her peers before being identified with a learning disability. In this case, by the time of identification, the student has met with repeated failure.

The Individuals Disabilities Education Act (IDEA), the federal law for students with disabilities, has placed much emphasis on reading fluency and reading comprehension. In fact, IDEA recognizes that several assessments are needed to determine if a student is eligible for special-education services or services related to specific learning disabilities. Wolf and Katzir-Cohen (2001, p. 219) refer to reading fluency as a level of accuracy and rate where decoding is relatively effortless; where oral reading is smooth and accurate with correct prosody, and where attention can be allocated to comprehension.

Because so much emphasis is being placed on reading fluency and reading comprehension, it appears that the constructs of emotional intelligence do indeed provide a framework for understanding emotional processes in students with reading disabilities. Studies show that the constructs related to emotional intelligence in reading are understood to affect students' academic achievement. It is also believed that, by regulating a student's emotional reactions in the reading environment, the teacher may in fact increase reading fluency and motivation (Pellitter, 2006).

Another component of reading is reading comprehension—the process of gaining meaning from the text. Reading comprehension is an important ability for secondary students with learning disabilities to possess because of the tremendous amounts of text students are required to read in content-area classes. Regardless of their disabilities, adolescents with reading disabilities are required to read a variety of texts (expository and narrative). Most high-school students with learning disabilities have the majority of their classes in general education and are expected to meet the same curricular demands as their peers. As cited by Lenz and Hughs (1990), secondary texts are written at the reading levels ranging from 10th- to 17th-grade levels. Studies show that the average reading level for high-school students with learning disabilities is approximately at the 4th-grade level (Alley & Deshler, 1979). If students with learning disabilities are having difficulty with reading, it would seem reasonable for these students to have difficulty with self-regulation, leading them to become passive and/or dependent learners with low motivation (Pellitter, 2006).

Learning disabilities (LD) vary from person to person. While one student may have a deficiency in math, another student may experience a deficiency in reading. More than 2.8 million school children are diagnosed with learning disabilities. Despite the growing number of students diagnosed with learning disabilities and stigmatized by its label, educators are still seeking ways to teach students with learning disabilities (Dudley-Marling, 2004).

In addition to weak academic performance, students come to school with more social and behavioral problems than did the students of the past. Some of these problems may be in part the result of bad home environments, negative influences, exposure to violence, poor or absent role models, television, or the media. Whatever the reason, these problems affect academic success in reading as well as in the other content areas, which are critical to school success and adult competence. Social-emotional skills can help to address and lessen these problems.

It's a vicious spiral: social and behavioral problems can cause weak academic performance, and weak academic performance can lead to further social and emotional problems. Grolnick and Ryan's study (as cited in Dyson, 2003) reveals that primary difficulties in the academic domain place LD children at risk for social and emotional difficulties. Twenty-four to 52% percent of children are reported to have significant social and emotional difficulties. Therefore, schools need to address this concern. Social-emotional-skills instruction needs to be a permanent part of the school's curriculum (Deshler, 2005).

Students with learning disabilities encounter rejection or neglect by their peers. This neglect and rejection contributes to poor or low self-perception (Boudah & Weiss, 2002). Unfortunately, these students also encounter higher levels of emotional distress related to their difficulties than do their peers without disabilities, which leads to higher levels of emotional concerns, such as depression, anxiety, loneliness, and low self-esteem. The experiences of emotional distress, such as anxiety, fear, anger, or depression, decrease a child's ability to attend, learn, or concentrate (Gorman, 1999). As a result of these difficult feelings of frustration, failure, and inferiority, the deficiencies are intensified (Abrams, 1986).

Negative challenges greatly affect academic learning, achievement, performance, and, of course, retention. These emotions are motivating forces which arouse, sustain, and direct activity and influence learning. In fact, these emotions, which are significant to the learning process, influence a range of behaviors such as helping, negotiating, altruism, risk taking, and compliance (Isen, 1984). Prolonged negative emotions can disrupt the thinking and learning process. Conversely, positive emotions can enhance the learning process.

When looking at the learning process, schools must change and look at ways in which to incorporate effective emotional-intelligence competencies. Schools must change the way in which they deal with students. Harrington-Lueker (1997) asserts that schools which fail to broaden their definition of intelligence to include moral development and social development will ultimately shortchange students and short-circuit academic achievement. It is believed that poor social skills are responsible for much of our unemployment and underemployment. In comparison, high levels of social skills can lead to occupational success.

Individuals with severe reading difficulties comprise a significant portion of the adult population of the United States. Kirsch, Jungeblut, Jenkins, and Kolstad (1993) conducted one of the largest literacy studies ever, which included a sample of over 13,000 U.S. adults as well as additional samples from state and prison populations. It was projected from their results that 40 to 44 million Americans cannot perform the simplest reading task, which include identifying a specific piece of information in a brief news article, or writing their name on a form. Their results show that these individuals are far less likely to work full time, to earn adequate wages, or to vote. In fact, these individuals are far less likely to participate fully and productively in the 21st century. This important study profiled over 13,000 adults; one would have to wonder if these individuals were once students with specific learning disabilities and if a relationship existed between their emotional intelligence and academic achievement. It is believed that reading is essential to all academic core areas and emotional intelligence affects academic performance.

Methodology

Respondents

The purpose of this study was to explore the relationship between emotional intelligence and academic achievement, specifically in reading comprehension, in 10th -, 11th -, and 12th-grade students with learning disabilities at Dillard High School. A purposive sample was utilized in recruiting 47 10th -, 11th -, and 12th grade students with learning disabilities from this high school in the Wayne County School District. Twenty female and 27 male respondents participated in the study, representing a 100% response rate.

Formal written consent was obtained from the principal, the Institutional Review Board, parents, and students. The testing procedure was arranged with the principal and the respondents' English teacher. Only those students with learning disabilities according to federal and state guidelines were included in the study. Respondents were informed that participation was voluntary and that they could withdraw at any time during the study. They were informed that all information would be kept confidential. In an effort to maintain anonymity, each student was assigned a number, and each of the tests was color coded according to grade level. The testing began once instructions were clarified. Once both tests were completed and placed in the appropriate color-coded folders, the respondents' names from these instruments were omitted.

The tests were conducted in a classroom, which offered ideal conditions for group testing. Group testing did not exceed 15 participants. The examination team consisted of an examiner and proctor with at least 10 to 28 years of test administration experience. Examiners followed test administration guidelines.

Instrumentation

The Bar-On Emotional Intelligence Questionnaire and the Wide Range Achievement Test–Expanded (reading comprehension test) were utilized in examining the relationship between emotional intelligence and academic achievement in reading comprehension in high-school students with learning disabilities at Dillard High School. The Bar-On Emotional Quotient Inventory Youth Short Version (Bar-On EQ-i:YVS), a specific EI-testing device designed by Bar-On (2000), was used to measure emotional intelligence and reading comprehension. It consisted of 30 questions and could be administered in approximately 10 to 15 minutes. Each item had a choice of four responses ranging from "Not True of Me

(Never, Seldom)" to "Very Much True of Me (Very Often)" (Bar-On &

Parker, 2000). The respondent read a sentence and chose the answer that

best described him or her. The Bar-On EQ-i:YVS Technical Manual

(2000) provided the information and instructions for interpreting the

results of the emotional-intelligence survey.

The Wide Range Achievement Test–Expanded Group Assessment was

used to assess reading comprehension and could be administered within

one 50-minute class period. This test consisted of 45 short passages which

the respondent read and then answered a question about. The WRAT–

Expanded test was normed on students, ages 5 to 24 years, covering

college-age students with learning disabilities. The Level 5 Group

Assessment *Administration Manual* provided the information and

instructions needed to administer, score, and interpret the WRAT–

Expanded.

Summary of Findings

Five research questions were examined in determining the relationship

between emotional intelligence and reading comprehension in high-school

students with learning disabilities at Dillard High School. The following

questions were examined:

126

1. What is the relationship between emotional intelligence and reading comprehension in high-school students with learning disabilities at Dillard High School? The findings show that there is a significant relationship between the total emotional-intelligence score and reading comprehension.

2. What is the relationship between emotional intelligence and reading comprehension and gender in high-school students with learning disabilities at Dillard High School? The findings revealed a very slight difference in scores. However, this very slight difference was not statistically meaningful. Emotional intelligence was not affected by gender.

3. What is the relationship between emotional intelligence and grade level in high-school students with learning disabilities at Dillard High School? The results of the study show that there is no significant difference in grade level and emotional intelligence.

4. What is the relationship between reading comprehension and gender in high- school students with learning disabilities at Dillard High School? The findings show that there is no significant relationship between reading comprehension and gender.

5. What is the relationship between reading comprehension and grade level in high-school students with learning disabilities at Dillard High

School? The findings show that there is not relationship between grade level and reading comprehension.

Discussion and Interpretations of Findings

Research Question 1

What is the relationship between emotional intelligence and reading comprehension in high-school students with learning disabilities at Dillard High School?

In this study, the Pearson Product-Moment Correlation Coefficient was utilized in determining the relationship between the total EQ (emotional intelligence) score and reading comprehension. The results indicate a strong relationship between total score and reading comprehension. This means that 81% of the variance in reading comprehension can be explained by the variance in emotional intelligence. The total score for EQ ranged from 55 to 93, with a mean of 71.60. The total score for reading comprehension ranged from 2.0 to 26.0 with a mean of 11.96. The Cronback alpha reliability estimate for the EQ was 0.710 indicating a moderately reliable instrument for the group under study. A significant correlation of ($r = 0.90$, $p = 0.00$) was obtained.

The findings address the relationship between emotional intelligence and reading comprehension in high-school students with learning disabilities. The total EQ score (emotional intelligence) gives an indication of how emotionally and socially mature the respondent is in general. A total EQ score that ranges between 70 and 79 is considered to be very low, demonstrating extremely underdeveloped emotional and social capacity with considerable room for improvement (Bar-On, 2000).

It has been established that emotional intelligence affects reading comprehension and that students with learning disabilities have serious academic and social deficiencies. The findings of this study show students who obtained high EQ scores also scored high in reading comprehension and students who received low EQ scores also scored low in reading comprehension. These findings suggest that one affects the other. In my opinion, there is a need to incorporate emotional-intelligence skills, such as self-regulation, self-awareness, and empathy, in the curriculum to improve students' emotional well being.

Research Question 2

What is the relationship between emotional intelligence and gender of students with learning disabilities at Dillard High School?

Popular literature has created an interest in gender differences associated with emotional intelligence. The popularity of works such as *Men Are from Mars and Women Are from Venus* (Gray, 1993) is indicative of this fascination. Conventional wisdom suggests that men and women have different styles of emotional intelligence, which are in part related to traditional notions of what is believed to be gender-specific roles. It has also been established that many more males than females are identified with learning disabilities (Friend, 2006). For that reason, most studies focus on male subjects while little is known about female subjects with learning disabilities and even less about gender differences. Even though most studies seem to address male subjects, this researcher explored gender as well.

It is reported that women tend to demonstrate greater compassion and emotional maturity than men. This could be in part due to the way girls and boys are socialized. Girls are taught to show their feelings and emotions, and to express themselves. Meanwhile, boys are told that men do not cry; they are taught to be strong and not show emotions. Studies by Bernet (1996a) and Sutarso, Baggert, Sutarso, and Tapia (1996) found that women tend to demonstrate greater compassion and empathy than men. This literature, however, is mixed in terms of differences on self-awareness and self-control.

In a study conducted by Bernet (1996b) using an instrument designed to operationalize some of the constructs of emotional intelligence, females demonstrated only slightly greater abilities in social-emotional intelligence, greater doubt about feelings and decisions, and less emphasis on the intellect. The educational field has yet to reach a consensus regarding gender differences in emotional intelligence.

The results of this study suggest that gender did not seem to have any relationship with emotional intelligence in high-school students with learning disabilities. On the Bar-On the mean score for males was 71.66, and the total mean for females was 71.60. This very slight difference was not statistically meaningful. Since a significant relationship was not found, and since emotional intelligence is considered an alterable variable that can be taught and learned, embedding it into the curriculum may have great potential benefits for both male and female students with learning disabilities.

Research Question 3

What is the relationship between emotional intelligence and grade level of students with learning disabilities at Dillard High School?

To determine if there was a relationship between grade levels, a one-way ANOVA statistical procedure was performed. The mean for Bar-On Grade 10 was 73.50; for Grade 11, 71.30; and for Grade 12, 69.70. The results of this study show grade level did not significantly correlate with emotional intelligence.

Research Question 4

What is the relationship between reading comprehension and gender in high-school students with learning disabilities at Dillard High School?

To investigate whether gender affected reading comprehension in high-school students with learning disabilities, a *t* test was performed. The results from this statistical procedure indicate gender did not seem to affect reading comprehension. The mean was 12.50 for males and 11.10 for females. Although the mean score for males was slightly higher, the score was not statistically significant.

Research Question 5

What is the relationship between reading comprehension and grade level in high- school students with learning disabilities at Dillard High School?

To investigate whether grade level affected reading comprehension in high-school students with learning disabilities at Dillard High School, a one-way ANOVA was performed , resulting in a mean of 10.50 for Grade 10, 12.20 for Grade 11, and 13.10 for Grade 12. This means that grade level did not seem to affect reading comprehension.

Conclusion

It has been established that students with learning disabilities have many challenges to overcome. As a result of these perpetual challenges, failures, frustrations, aggressions, and other behaviors, their academic and social problems intensify. Despite these obstacles which include repeated academic, social, and social-emotional challenges, students with learning disabilities can achieve.

Reading comprehension is essential to academic achievement in all core areas. However, personal observation is that reading comprehension and emotional intelligence share a strong relationship in students with learning disabilities. Reading comprehension is vital to one's success in life, and so is emotional intelligence. Based on the findings of this study, it appears that both reading comprehension and emotional intelligence share a strong relationship. Since reading comprehension and emotional intelligence share a strong relationship, one affecting the other, emotional-intelligence competence skills should be embedded into the school's curricula.

If students with learning disabilities are to be prepared for today's academic challenges, the educational paradigm must be broadened to include emotional competence skills. If students with learning disabilities are to be prepared for today's academic and social challenges, the paradigm of education must change to educate the whole child by teaching those skills that are vital to life's success.

Recommendations

It has been postulated that success depends on several intelligences and the control of emotions. Goleman (1995) posits that IQ alone is no longer the measure for success and that IQ counts only for 20%, while the rest is determined by emotional intelligence and luck. Since emotional intelligence is considered essential for today's success, its components should be taught in the classrooms. Since there is a significant relationship between emotional intelligence and reading comprehension, and reading is considered vital to all core areas, emotional-intelligence skills must be integrated into the overall school curricula. By teaching emotional-intelligence skills, reading comprehension and academic success will increase while some negative behaviors and academic failure will decrease.

Emotional Intelligence in Schools

The primary responsibility of the teachers has been to facilitate learning by helping students to reach their optimal level of academic functioning. However, students are confronted with far more social-emotional and academic challenges than ever before. Evidence shows that children and youth who demonstrate adequate social-emotional skills (emotional intelligence) are more likely to experience academic success and find acceptance with others. They are more emotionally well adjusted, and possess a higher level of self-esteem and self-confidence (Elksnin & Elksnin, 2005). On the other hand, children and youth who do not possess these social skills are more likely to experience difficulty, to be rejected, suffer mental-health problems, eventually drop out of school, and be unemployed during adult life (Elksnin, 1995, 1998, 2001).

Teachers on a daily basis integrate rules and management strategies into their classrooms, emphasizing acceptable classroom conduct. Then they proceed to teach the cognitive curriculum, but delivery of instruction is often interrupted by some students' negative behavior or student apathy. In general, the social-emotional needs of teenagers are not being met and, despite instructional strategies, students fail to achieve academically. Burdened by emotional processes that interfere with learning and by repeated failures, students often demonstrate acts of aggression, anger, or frustration. Social-emotional learning programs are designed to promote emotional-intelligence skills; addressing students' emotional and social needs can promote academic performance as well as good citizenship.

It is also believed that providing students with social and emotional education will decrease the likelihood of students becoming involved in risky behaviors such as violence, substance abuse, and early unprotected sex. It is believed that schools are the setting in which preventive efforts should take place (Graczyk et al., 2000). However, personal observation shows students with learning disabilities are overwhelmed with repeated failures and the stigma of being classed as "LD." These emotions also stand in the way of achievement. Unless the classroom becomes a positive environment where emotional-intelligence competencies are embedded into the classroom and students with learning disabilities can feel positive about themselves, these students will continue to be unmotivated and uninterested in learning. The concept of learning disabilities is not new. It has been debated for years, and most educators will agree that a new educational paradigm for preparing children with learning disabilities must be near at hand.

The results of this study have the potential to be used by both special-education and general-education teachers as they develop plans for student academic growth. Teachers would be able to incorporate emotional intelligence learning through literature as well as other disciplines. Because students are with their teachers for the majority of the school day, the opportunity to reach children with and without learning disabilities incorporating emotional intelligence skills may have tremendous potential.

Every child enters the world with a passion to learn. As educators, we can promote or extinguish that desire to learn. In order to assist students in reaching their full potential, teachers must continue to take risks and try new techniques. By taking risks, trying new techniques, and exploring new technologies, teachers may be able to turn a child's talents along with his passion for learning into a powerful force.

School Ancillary Support

School social workers and school psychologists have a unique opportunity to integrate social-emotional learning into group intervention settings. Students with learning disabilities need to be taught how to identify and solve social problems. Well-developed problem-solving ability enables children to determine how to use social skills, when to use social skills, and where to use them. School social workers and school psychologists would be able to utilize the problem-solving and social-emotional training when implementing small group settings for students at risk.

Educational Leadership Implications

Leading change is one of the most important, complex, and difficult tasks of school leadership (Fullan, 1993). According to Rauch and Behling (1984 p.46), "leadership is the process of influencing the activities of an organized group toward goal achievement." However, Schein (1992) posits that leadership is the ability to step outside the culture, to start evolutionary-change processes that are more adaptive. Richards and Engle (1986) believe that leadership is about articulating visions, embodying values, and creating the environment within which things can be accomplished. Educational leadership is positioned to empower teachers and the entire staff with the opportunity to implement instructional strategies for the development of students. It is the school's leadership responsibility to foster collaborative initiatives for both the school and the community.

This study has potential benefits for leadership and dynamic-change agents. School leadership has the ability to foster collaborative initiatives for both the school and community. Whether fostering emotional-intelligence learning at the local school level or district, educating the "whole" child is necessary. Holistic education would involve fostering academics and emotional-intelligence skills, as well as extracurricula activities. The time for holistic teaching and learning has arrived.

Leadership and Church Organizations

Church leadership and its departmental directors are positioned to implement instructional strategies and workshops for children, youth, and young adults as well as adult members of their congregation. Church leaders have a captive audience that most likely will be receptive to enhancing their social-emotional skills. Since emotional-intelligence skills can be learned and are considered critical for success, incorporating the components of emotional intelligence may prove beneficial to the members of the church at large. The components of emotional intelligence may be effectively implemented through youth ministries, as well as in other outreach ministries. This study has potential benefits for church organizations and the community at large.

Parental Involvement

The involvement of parents in the lives of their youth is of the utmost importance. It is the home where children are provided with social and emotional skills. All children have basic needs that must be met if they are to grow up into responsible, caring, informed, and contributing members of society. Parental support and active involvement are essential for students to experience academic and social success. Parents are often concerned with academic success but do not realize the correlation between academic achievement and emotional intelligence. Parents may need to be educated regarding the components of emotional intelligence and its relationship with success. Conjecture is that it is not the teachers' responsibility to teach children those skills that should be taught at home. However, students come to school with both social and academic needs. Each of these deficiencies appears to affect the other. Therefore, it is essential that parents and teachers collaborate, working together toward a common goal. That common goal is society's customers.

Standardized Assessment

Various kinds of standardized assessments are used yearly to test students with learning disabilities. Some of these assessments are the same assessments used for testing the general-education population. Since students' academic progress is always a measurable concern, this study may be useful for standardized-test developers. It would be helpful if test developers would include a section in one of the standardized tests administered to students, to determine areas that could benefit from intervention strategies. Since academic achievement has a correlation to emotional intelligence, it would be beneficial to discover a student's strength as well as the student's emotional intelligence.

Office of Specialized Student Services for Students with Special Needs

This study has the potential to be used by professionals who identify and develop goals and objectives for students with special needs as they transition to adult life. The Special Education Department for the State of Michigan has the responsibility of developing and implementing long-range and short-term goals for students with special needs. When the designers of the Individual Education Plans (IEPs) implement plans for the special-needs child, it would be worthwhile for them to incorporate both social-emotional and academic goals and objectives.

Future Direction of Research

This study on the relationship between emotional intelligence and reading comprehension in high-school students with learning disabilities was conducted using a purposive sample. This purposive sample consisted of a total of 47 female and male respondents from a large high school in the Wayne County School District. The results of this study indicate a strong correlation between emotional intelligence and reading comprehension. Several limitations of this study should be noted. First, the sample was relatively small and restricted to a single high school. Replications in other high schools are necessary before the results can be generalized. Second, the sample was drawn from students who were diagnosed as having a disability in reading. Therefore, only the reading subscale assessment was administered. Third, age was not used as a variable. Last, the study should be replicated using 9th-, 10th-, 11th-, and 12th-grade students.

It is also recommended that teachers, parents, and administrators be informed about the components of emotional intelligence. As educators, we need to change the way we think about teaching students with and without learning disabilities. Emotional intelligence and reading comprehension (a skill which is considered key to fundamental learning) work in parallel and significant ways. Realizing that it is no longer enough to provide students with an education that only emphasizes core subjects, and that one's emotional intelligence is a determinant of one's success, schools need to embrace and integrate a new educational paradigm that is geared toward educating the whole child. Integrating emotional-intelligence competence skills in the curriculum would require designing an academic curriculum that also addresses the following:

1. Self-Awareness: identifying feelings, emotions, and strengths.

2. Self-Regulation: managing emotions and solving problems and conflicts appropriately.

3. Motivation: setting realistic, obtainable goals and working toward those goals.

4. Empathy: being sensitive and respectful to others.

5. Social Skills: working cooperatively and collaboratively, valuing others' opinions for diversity, and being aware of social situations.

Research shows that schools that integrate emotional-intelligence competence skills into their curriculum have seen worthwhile results in decreasing student aggression, student violence, drug use, and other forms of negative social behaviors. In order to prepare our youth for the workforce and to be productive members of society, schools must change the way in which we educate our children. Additionally, it is essential that educators, administrators, and parents are made aware of emotional intelligence and how it affects life's success.

Although helping children reach their optimal level of functioning has been challenging, achieving the kind of balance that includes academic and emotional skills is critical. If America's children are to become literate, responsible, caring, problem-solving, and contributing adults, then leadership, educators, the community, and legislature must band together to embrace the common goal of educating the whole child. Educating the whole child for life's success means changing the school's curriculum.

CHAPTER SIX

The Effective Emotionally-Intelligent Teacher

"The mediocre teacher tells.
The good teacher explains.
The superior teacher demonstrates, and
The great teacher inspires."
— *Grady Jones, Principal*

What is the effective emotionally intelligent teacher? She/he is an effective teacher with the ability to teach, develop, and enhance emotional intelligence skills.

"Educating the mind without educating the heart is no education at all."
— *Aristotle*

Chapters 1-5 presented research entitled "The Relationship between Emotional Intelligence and Reading Comprehension in High School Students with Learning Disabilities." Because empirical evidence suggests that traditional intelligence is not enough for *"What lies in our power to do, lies in our power not to do" — Aristotle* one's life success and that educating the whole child is essential for one to succeed in today's global society, emotional intelligence must be embedded in the educational curriculum. We, as educators, must do all that we can to prepare students to succeed not only in the classroom, not only academically, but in life; we must do all that we can do to prepare students for life's success.

As teachers, we can agree that emotions are at the center of attention, motivation, memory, achievement, behavior, and relationships (Mayer & Salovey, 1997).

Research reveals that children who participate in emotional-intelligence and social-competence programs had improved problem-solving skills, improved peer relationships, better impulse control, and improved social behaviors. Given these results, I would like to share a few resources for integrating emotional-intelligence competencies in the classroom.

You are probably wondering, "How on earth will I find the time to integrate additional skills into my already overloaded curriculum?" Integrating emotional-intelligence skills or competencies can easily and most simply be taught in the English curriculum (English literature; reading; short stories; movies, and plays). With a little creativity, teachers, while presenting lessons about artists, scientists, and musicians, can use those famous people's biographies and challenges as a means of integrating EI skills into the classroom.

What makes an effective Emotional-Intelligence Teacher? The Emotional-Intelligence Teacher uses a systematic process of teaching lifelong skills and emotional concepts that foster well-being, improved academic achievement, and improved social relationships. Perhaps you may say that this approach is much too challenging to adopt at this point in your teaching career. Perhaps you may feel that this is not for you to attempt because your curriculum and class syllabus are already set. Perhaps you are thinking you do not get paid to do what a parent should be doing and it is not your responsibility to teach children social skills. Given societies' ills, why not assume this responsibility? Isn't teaching about preparing students to succeed in life? You may not receive immediate gratification, but we all have our stories about the caring and nurturing teacher we had "back then" who is still making an impact on our lives *now*. Why deny your pupils the opportunity to feel the same way about you one day?

"I never teach my pupils; I only attempt to provide the conditions in which they can learn" — Albert Einstein

So what does an emotional intelligent classroom look like? Just what criteria are used in determining an effective teacher? What measuring stick is used to determine what is considered effective teaching? What makes a teacher effective? Should teachers' effectiveness be determined by how well their students are prepared or their students' ability to read; or by the teachers' own communication skills; knowledge and ability to convey materials; knowledge of multiple intelligence or student learning styles; knowledge of emotional intelligence or student preparation; or by their many years of service?

Certainly, effective teachers are teachers who are prepared and knowledgeable and who are themselves teachable, flexible, and emotionally intelligent. Effective teachers, without a doubt, and without contractual agreement, extend themselves beyond the extra mile. (And going the extra mile sometimes includes being a parent, counselor, nurturer, motivator, initiator, psychologist, nurse, and more.) Yet, oftentimes, teachers are vilified, the least respected, and, in many instances, the most underpaid.

So what makes a teacher effective? Teacher effectiveness and effective teaching can be characterized in numerous ways, but this chapter will only highlight a few.

Skills in Using, Evaluating, and Adapting Instructional Materials

An effective teacher possesses numerous skills, including skills in using, evaluating, and adapting instructional material. According to Brooks (1993), assessment tools should be used to enhance both the student's learning and the teacher's understanding of the student's current understanding. Before instruction begins, educational-assessment tools should be administered to determine the student's entry level. Educational assessments include oral responses, individual written responses and group written responses. These educational assessments may be criterion reference measurement (formal assessments and teacher-made informal tests to determine the student's entry level). The assessment tools, however, should not be used as accountability tools or methods, which may encourage some students to feel good and others to give up (Brooks 1993).

An effective teacher uses a variety of assessments, to determine a student's entry level and to determine the best instructional strategies to implement for each student. The purpose of course, of the readiness assessment is to determine which skills the student has mastered and which skills need to be taught.

Assessment instruments would be used to 1) identify areas of strength and weaknesses, 2) identify basis skills within those areas that have or have not been mastered. 3) identify instructional goals and objectives that should be met by the student in order to achieve or master a specific level, 4) provide the language appropriate for stating objectives, and 5) provide data that will support other pertinent information needed for referral or diagnostic purposes.

An Effective Teacher/Instructor with Skills in Instructional Management to Accommodate Individual Variability

Before the instructional process begins, an effective teacher must have effective classroom-management skills. The effective teacher/mentor must be able to establish a rapport with the students, clarify expectations, and establish classroom norms. In order to have students embrace classroom norms, it would be helpful to allow the students to engage in providing norms for the classroom. To clarify student and teacher expectations, a course syllabus is essential. Once student and teacher rapport is established and classroom norms and objectives have been communicated, the learning process can begin.

When looking at the learning process and planning relative instruction, it is important to consider instructional strategies, which take into, account multiple intelligences. Gardner (1983) posits that students demonstrate multiple intelligences, which include the following:

1. Linguistic intelligence ("word smart")
2. Logical mathematical intelligence ("number/reasoning, smart")
3. Spatial intelligence ("picture smart")
4. Bodily-kinetic intelligence ("body smart")

5. Musical intelligence ("music smart")

6. Interpersonal intelligence ("people smart")

7. Intrapersonal intelligence ("self-smart")

8. Naturalist intelligence ("nature smart")

These eight intelligences are believed to affect today's classroom, as they are present in students of varying ages, cultures, and socioeconomic strata.

Gardner's multiple intelligences included components of emotional intelligence (intrapersonal, interpersonal, and people skills), which are considered to be determinants of life's success. As a result, an effective teacher should use a wide variety of instructional strategies to present lessons to accommodate student individualities and learning styles.

Four Major Learning Modalities

There are four major modalities of learning, and integrating them into lesson-plan development is essential.

Table 8

Four Styles of Learning

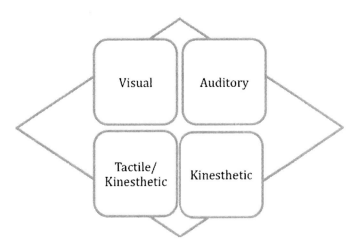

The Auditory Learner prefers listening; learn best by hearing; have the ability to memorize what they hear; learn through presentations, enjoys music, speaking, and plays.

The Visual Learner with their visual preferences, learn best through the use of visuals (charts, pictures, graphs, diagrams, videos, flip charts, and hand-outs).

The Kinesthetic Learner, learn best by writing things down. The Kinesthetic learner enjoys activities that allow movement, the use of manipulatives, designing and building. Kinesthetic learners may demonstrate high energy levels.

The Tactile Learners prefer hands – on approach. They are usually artistic in nature and enjoy doodling. Tactile learners do well with projects, demonstrations or labs and prefer "doing" rather than watching or listening.

Teaching and modeling provide the basis for true leadership. Maxwell (1999) asserts that the number-one management principle in the world is that people do what people see. According to the Hunter Model (Elements of Effective Instruction), effective teaching/mentoring requires a plan. She postulates that there are seven steps for effective lesson planning:

1. Objectives

2. Set (the hook)

3. Standard Expectations

4. Teaching (input, modeling, checking for understanding)

5. Guided Practice

6. Closure

7. Independent Practice

Input, modeling and checking for understanding should be included as key components of lesson planning. If you break down teaching into those three steps, there are *nine* steps.

If the above outline is prepared, the teacher would have a clear understanding of the objectives, what standards of performance are to be expected, and when pupils will be held accountable. The teacher would be able to focus student attention on the lesson, thus creating an organizing framework for the ideas, principles, or information. The teacher would be able to model, provide input, and check for understanding. The teacher would be able to guide each student through a new learning activity or exercise, and, at the same time, the teacher would be ale to bring the lesson to a close by asking questions and briefly summarizing and clarifying the lesson.

An effective teacher also uses cooperative learning to maximize student achievement. It has been reported that collaborative learning enhances student achievement. The term "collaborative learning" refers to an instructional method in which students at various performance levels work together in small groups, assisting each other in achieving a common goal. According to Johnson and Johnson (1986), when students work in small groups, actively engaged in exchanging ideas, it increases the interest of the group and promotes critical thinking.

Instructional Strategies may include but are not limited to cooperative learning, art activities, role playing, reflections, music, the use of media and technology, peer tutoring, essays, debates, and more.

Vgotsky (1978) posits that individuals imitate modeled behavior from personally observing others, the environment, and mass media. He also believes that students are capable of performing at high intellectual levels when asked to work in collaborative situations compared to when asked to work individually. When students collaboratively help each other, they develop skills that are essential to building a supportive community. As a result of this collaborative effort, the students' performance level increases. This collaborative support also enhances the students' self-esteem. Collaboration, team building and social skills are components of emotional intelligence.

In order to keep students engaged and the motivation levels high, Brooks & Brooks (1999) assert that teachers should structure lessons around foundational ideas, pose problems of emerging relevance, and value students' points of view.

Establishing an Emotionally Intelligent Classroom

Your current classroom can be enhanced, by integrating emotional-intelligence competency skills. An emotionally intelligent classroom should begin with a curriculum that integrates real life experiences or situations. Incorporating the components of emotional intelligence (which include self-awareness, empathy, self-regulation/motivation, and handling relationships) is critical to one's success.

Emotional Intelligence at a Glance

Figure 1

Five Components of Emotional Intelligence

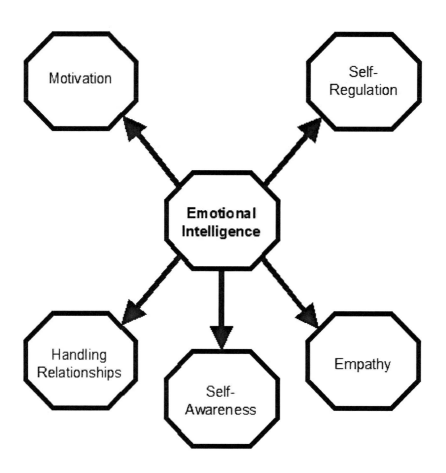

Emotional Intelligence at a Glance: Hallmarks and Characteristics

EI	Hallmark	Characteristics
Self-Awareness	Ability to recognize and understand your moods, emotions, and drives as well as their efforts on others Being smart about what we are feeling	Self-confidence Realistic self-assessment Self-deprecating sense of humor "Anyone can become angry – that is easy, but to be angry with the right person, to the right degree, at the right time, for the right purpose, and in the right way – that is not easy" (Gibbs, 1995)
Self-Regulation	Ability to control or redirect disruptive impulses and moods Propensity to suspend judgment – to think before acting	Trustworthiness and integrity Comfort with ambiguity Openness to change

EI	Hallmark	Characteristics
Motivation	Passion to work for reasons that go beyond money or status Propensity to pursue goals with energy and persistence	Strong drive to achieve Optimism, even in the face of failure Organizational commitment
Empathy	Ability to understand the emotional make-up of other people Skill in treating people according to their emotional reactions	Expertise in building and retaining talent Cross-cultural sensitivity Service to others
Social Skills/ Handling Relationships	Proficiency in managing relationships and building networks Ability to find common-ground and build rapport	Effectiveness in leading change Persuasiveness Effectiveness in leading change Expertise in building and leading teams

Reprinted by permission of Harvard Business Review. From "What Makes a Leader" by Daniel Goleman, Jan. 2004, Copyright ©2004

Basic Empowerment Strategies for Creating an Emotionally Intelligent Learning Environment

Figure 2

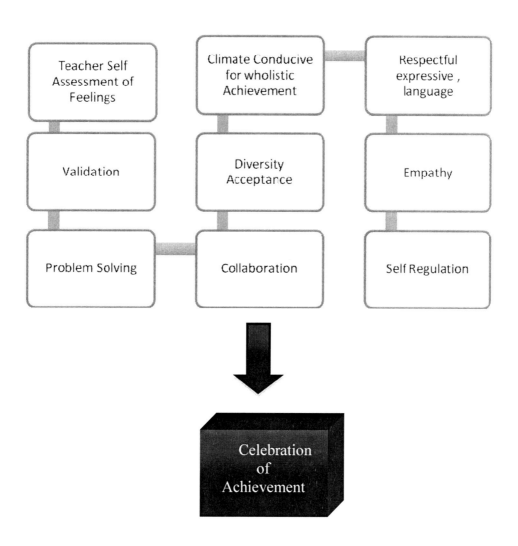

Personal Reflection and EI Enhancement

The EQ-i is a scientifically validated test of emotional intelligence and is used by many organizations to predict, improve, and develop individual and organization performance. The BarOn Emotional Intelligence Inventory (EQ-i) is used globally and may be administered upon request. Meanwhile, why not engage in a bit of personal reflection?

What Does Personal Reflection and Self-Assessment Have to Do with Teaching?

Let us first begin by considering the following few familiar quotes.

He who knows others is learned;

He who knows himself is wise.

— Lao-tzu, *Tao te Ching*

"He who dares to teach must never cease to learn."

— John Cotton Dana

"*If* your emotional abilities aren't in hand,

If you don't have self-awareness,

If you are not able to manage your distressing emotions,

If you can't have empathy and have effective relationships,

Then, no matter how smart you are,

You are not going to get very far."

— Daniel Goleman

Steps and Strategies for Establishing an Emotionally Intelligent Classroom

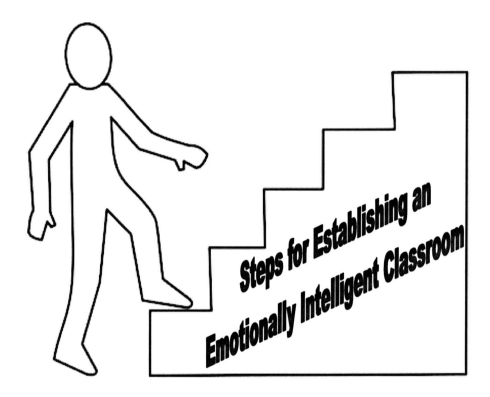

Let us begin with Step 1.

Assessing Your Own Emotions

Self Regard

1. List those skills and abilities that describe your proficiency. _____

   _____

   _____

   _____

2. Are there any skills and/or abilities about which you feel less proficient? _____

   _____

   _____

3. Are there any areas in which you would like to improve? _____

   _____

   _____

   _____

4. How do you use your strengths and proficiencies to inspire others?

   _____

   _____

   _____

(See the review of EI competencies at the end of this section.)

Emotional Self-Awareness

1. What are your triggers for negative emotions? _____
   _____
   _____

2a. Traffic was bad when you were coming into school this morning, and now the principal asked you to cover a class. Johnny comes in with a tantrum. Jane comes in crying, and Laya comes in noisily, throwing her books on the desk. Describe your emotions. _____
   _____
   _____

2b. Describe what you are feeling and why you feel that way. _____
   _____
   _____

2c. How do you handle this classroom situation? _____
   _____
   _____

2d. How has stressful situations affected your decision making, or planning?_____
   _____

(See the review of EI competencies at the end of this section.)

Empathy

1. What does this particular emotional-intelligence competency (empathy) mean to you? _____

    _____

    _____

    _____

2. Differentiate between empathy and sympathy. _____

    _____

    _____

    _____

2a. How do you listen to others?_____ Are you easily distracted when listening to others? _____.

2b. What signals do you send when others or talking to you?_____

2c. What do you do to celebrate others?

    _____

    _____

(See the review of EI competencies at the end of this section.)

Stress Tolerance

1. When stressful situations occur, how do you keep from becoming anxious or agitated or from being overwhelmed? _____

    _____

    _____

    _____

    _____

2. When unpleasant situations or events occur, what do you do to remain calm? _____

    _____

    _____

    _____

    _____

2a. How has stressful situations affected your decision-making, or planning?

    _____

    _____

    _____

(See the review of EI competencies at the end of this section.)

166

Impulse Control

1. You are trying to get to work or trying to be on time for an appointment, and the driver ahead of you is not driving the speed limit. What would you do? _____

   _____

   _____

   _____

   _____

   _____

2. What would you do to remain calm or not overreact? _____

   _____

   _____

   _____

   _____

   _____

2a. Do you make decisions to take on a project before fully understanding, or conceptualizing?

   _____

   _____

   _____

(See the review of EI competencies at the end of this section.)

Adaptability

"Enjoying success requires the ability to adapt. Only by being open to change will you have true opportunity to get the most from your talent."
— *Nolan Ryan*

1. Your administrator has increased your responsibilities. With these new responsibilities, you have difficulty meeting a deadline. What would you do to solve this situation? _____

    _____

    _____

    _____

    _____

2. How do you adjust your emotions, feelings, and thoughts to meet unscheduled deadlines? _____

    _____

    _____

    _____

    _____

(See the review of EI competencies at the end of this section.)

General Mood

"Optimism is the faith that leads to achievement. Nothing can be done without hope and confidence" — Helen Keller

1. When dealing with adverse situations, how do you maintain a positive attitude? _____

   _____

   _____

   _____

   _____

2. At your lowest moment, what is your outlook on life? _____

   _____

   _____

   _____

   _____

(See the review of EI competencies at the end of this section.)

Notes for Personal Development

EI Competencies in Review

Self Regard: Teachers or individuals with positive or good self-regard are aware of their strengths, weaknesses, limitations, and possibilities.

Individuals who score well in this area of self-regard know their own proficiencies and limitations

Emotional Self-Awareness: If you are emotionally self-aware, you are able to identify, label, and manage your feelings while taking care not to displace your feelings. Teachers or individuals who have good emotional self- awareness are able to identify or label how they are feeling and why. Teachers who score well in emotional intelligence recognize how their feelings affect their performance and understand what affect their feelings have on others. Individuals who score well in this area are aware of their emotions and are able to express their feelings, appropriately.

This competency is the foundation for EQ-i skills. If one is in touch with his/her own feelings and emotions, has the ability to label those feelings and emotions, and can understand/explain why s/he is feeling that way, then that individual has the ability to interact and work with others.

Empathy: Teachers or individuals with empathy are able to place themselves in their students' skin—to sense students' feelings, needs, and concerns. Individuals who score well in empathy are able to see things from someone else's perspective. Individuals who score well in this area are sensitive to others, demonstrate an appreciation of others, and are able to differentiate between empathy and sympathy.

Adaptability: Teachers or individuals with this competency are flexible in handling change. They are able to shift priorities without distress. Individuals with this competency are able to adapt or adjust methods or tactics to meet change or circumstances. They are able to shift gears, adapting circumstances to fit the need.

Individuals with good scores in this area are flexible and are able to cope with change, unforeseen challenges, or circumstances that life brings us.

Stress Tolerance: Teachers or individuals with this competency are able to manage stress effectively and positively. They are able to manage their emotions as well as the emotions of their students. Individuals with this competency are able to cope with stress without falling to pieces.

Individuals who score high in the area of stress tolerance are able to handle stressful situations in a positive and calm manner without "losing" it.

Individuals with good scores in this area demonstrate patience and are able to control themselves in stressful situations.

Self-Regulation: Teachers and individuals with this competency have the ability to manage their impulsive feelings, remaining composed during difficult times.

General Mood: Teachers with this competency have a positive perspective on life. These individuals are able to view life's adversities positively, seeing challenges as opportunities to succeed. These individuals view life optimistically and are usually happy

Individuals with good scores in this area have an optimistic outlook on life. These individuals are usually happy with their lives and are able to put things in their proper perspective.

Empower students to achieve academically and emotionally in a safe environment.

Create a safe classroom that is conducive to holistic learning—one in which students will feel safe, comfortable, and unthreatened, one that is attractive and colorful. Through positive reinforcement, educate the whole child so that students are unafraid to have a difference of opinion and to express it.

Empower students to achieve through expressive language (self-awareness)

Journaling is an excellent strategy to use for allowing students to engage in reflective writing (writing about their emotions, labeling their feels without being challenged) or expressive writing (commenting on class discussions and projects, role playing). It is also a great strategy to assist them in settling down before the lesson begins. Set aside a few minutes for positive thinking and communicating.

Empower students to achieve through validation

Using acceptance, concern, empathy and caring will go a long way. Positive affirmations foster a positive mindset, self-esteem, and confidence. Establish a "Yes, I Can" and "Yes, We Can" classroom.

Empower students to achieve by recognizing diversity

What does this mean? Respecting and accepting differences without ridicule. Accepting relativity without ethnicity. Helping students to recognize they are important and that their opinions really, matter.

Perhaps you can teach diversity using plays and role-playing activities. Invite guest speakers from various ethnic groups. Provide opportunities and lessons, whereby students celebrate and appreciate differences. Commemorating holidays of different cultures and pointing out the various historical contributions that different groups have made is beneficial in teaching and celebrating diversity. Additionally, celebrate your students' achievements and special events.

Empower students to achieve through empathy

What does this mean? Teach students to be sensitive to others. Use real-life situations to demonstrate active and genuine interest. This is a skill that is the foundation for moral development. If students do not develop empathy, they may later be viewed as callous adults.

Empower students to achieve through problem solving

Use essential techniques to teach problem solving or conflict resolution by having students demonstrate an understanding of the problem and getting them to select strategies to solve problems. Have students provide different ways to resolve conflicts without negativity, name-calling, verbal/emotional abuse, or violence. Generate real life lessons and activities that teach conflict resolution and problem solving. For the journal-writing assignment, assign a Problem of the Day.

Empower students to achieve through collaboration

This competency also involves team building. Demonstrate ways that students can exchange shared ideas to identify problems, make decisions, and achieve goals. Demonstrate ways of compromising while keeping focused on a desired goal. Show the significance of clear communication and how having different perspectives and views work toward common goals. Have students identify the "soft spots" or hurdles that may hinder progress and/or cause discomfort.

Generate a class atmosphere of Team Building

Demonstrate how working together on group projects can be accomplished. Using various modalities of teaching, recognize and identify students' various strengths and abilities to complete a group project. For instance, if the assignment is to have students work in groups to generate a book report on a particular short story, the composition of the group may include

1. A student who reads well and does not mind reading orally to benefit the students in the group, who may not read so well.

2. A student who has the ability to draw, who can make a visual presentation of the book report that will be presented.

3. A student who has the ability to make an oral presentation of the book report.

4. A student who has the ability to take notes or summarize the report

5. A student with computer skills who can type up the formal presentation, or generate a power point presentation that includes all of the group members names.

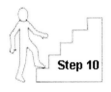

Generate a "Win-Win" Atmosphere whereby every student is able to achieve and experiences success!

Step 10

Using Literature to Teach EI and Social Learning Competencies

Whether your classroom is a general-education classroom or a classroom for students with special needs, emotional-intelligence competences can be taught. Yes, over time, and with commitment, emotional intelligence can be developed or even improved! Although all disciplines can integrate EI competencies into their classroom curriculum, an English Class or a Reading Class presents an ideal setting for teaching these competencies.

For literature classes, Table 9 includes a list of books and short stories that can be utilized in teaching those skills that, according to research, affect life's success. This list is by no means exhaustive; it merely provides a good starting point—a sampling of fiction and non-fiction that can be used for teaching EI competencies.

Following also, is a list of literary examples that can be used to develop lesson plans that address emotional-intelligence competencies.

Table 9

Literature Resources

Book or Short Story	Author	Emotional-Intelligence Competency	Identify Multiple Intelligences and Learning Modalities you would use to engage students
"Marigolds"	Eugenia Collier	Empathy Self-Regulation / Impulse Control Stress Tolerance Self-Awareness	Visual: Role Playing; power point presentation Kinesthetic: journaling Auditory: discussions; reading and being read to; debate
I Know Why Caged Bird Sings	Maya Angelo	Self –Awareness	Visual Kinesthetic Auditory Tactile
The Story of My Life *Out of the Dark* *Teacher*	Helen Keller Helen Keller Helen Keller	Self-Motivation Self-Motivation Self- Awareness Self-Motivation	Visual Kinesthetic Auditory Tactile
"Where Have You Gone, Charming Billy?"	Tim O'Brien	Self-Awareness	Visual Kinesthetic Auditory Tactile
"The Gift of the Magi"	O. Henry	Decision-Making Problem Solving	Visual Kinesthetic Auditory Tactile
"On Being Seventeen, Bright and Unable to Read"	David Raymond	Self-Motivation Self-Awareness Self-Regard	Visual Kinesthetic Auditory Tactile

"Marigolds" by Eugene Collier

Teaching emotional intelligence to young students can be quite challenging, yet, when EI is effectively integrated, the benefits are enormous. Short stories, movies, plays, role-playing, classroom "teachable moments," and other "real-life situations" provide an engaging and rich opportunity to prepare students for life's success. When emotional-intelligence competencies are embedded into the classroom's curriculum and structure, students' personal competence can be enhanced. However, one of the most powerful instructional modalities for teaching emotional intelligence and social competencies is modeling.

As a way of modeling one's behavior, "Marigolds" provides several teachable concepts. (And, although "Marigolds" is a popular short story, it is by no means the *only* short story that can be utilized to teach "soft skills."). Because of the rich vocabulary and emotions found in this short story, several emotional competencies can be examined.

The following is a brief analysis of Eugene Collier's "Marigolds":

> The story takes place during the Great Depression when unemployment and poverty have reached alarming heights. Elizabeth (the narrator), Joey (her brother), her father and mother; Miss Lottie, and John (Miss Lottie's son) are the characters.

The story provides a snapshot of the life of a young girl whose life was filled with poverty, complex family dynamics, and a sense of confusion and hopelessness. Elizabeth's sense of hopelessness, growing pains of adolescence, and lack of adult supervision by her mother reach a point of destruction.

Four major conflicts can be noted: 1) The feeling of entrapment—"Poverty was the cage in which we were all caged"; 2) disillusionment with the father whom Elizabeth looked up to as the pillar and head of the family but whom unemployment had reduced him to tears and despair; 3) Due to financial conditions, Elizabeth's mother was not around as Elizabeth experienced the growing pains of a young girl —"I feel again the chaotic emotions of adolescence, illusive as smoke, yet as real as potted geranium before me now"; 4) struggling with being a child while struggling to become a woman—"The world has lost its boundaries." These conflicts contributed to Elizabeth's rage and envy, driving her to destructive acts.   After the mean acts of destruction, she becomes ashamed and this seemingly, was the beginning of one of the emotional competencies - empathy (compassion).

You may think of beginning this lesson using its rich vocabulary. This lesson also affords an opportunity to write reflectively of times, they did something that they later regretted or would like to forget.

Application is Essential:
Lesson Plan Components at a Glance

Prior Teaching Preparation

Am I myself familiar with the subject and am I prepared to present it in a manner that the students can understand?

Objectives:

Using behavioral or performance-objective terms, state the objective.

1. Are the objectives clear, precise and obtainable?

2. Are the objectives measurable?

Rationale:

Provide the purpose of lesson.

Standard:

Indicate the stated curriculum framework, benchmark, or alignment for each objective.

Materials:

1. What materials are needed to successfully teach the lesson?

2. Have I reserved and tested the audiovisual equipment to ensure its functionality?

Procedures/Setting the Stage for Student Success

1. How will I introduce the lesson?

2. What will I do to generate a stimulating discussion?

3. What motivating questions will I ask?

4. What hook will I use to get the students' attention?

5. How will I model expected outcomes?

6. What will I do to ensure student readiness for the lesson?

7. What will I do to monitor an understanding of differentiated instruction?

8. What will I do to encourage reflective writing?

9. What assessments will I use for evaluation?

10. What will I do to summarize the lesson and bring closure?

11. Were specific instructions given for the assignment, test, or quiz?

Special Considerations

1. What accommodations do I have in place for students with special needs, students who would benefit from differentiated instruction, or students who require special consideration?

2. What do I have in place to keep early finishers from disturbing others?

3. What do I have in place for students who did not understand the concept? What will I do to re-teach the concept?

Enrichment:

What form of enrichment, instructional strategies, or projects will I use to enhance instruction?

Sample Lesson-Plan Templates

Lesson-Plan Template 1

Teacher		Course	
Room(s)		Date	
Standards		Material/Equip	

Standards: Indicate the Curriculum Framework Standard(s) that this lesson plan is designed to address.
Materials and Equipment = videotape, lab equipment, student worksheets, Power Points, etc.

	Objective[1]	Procedure[2]	Student Activity[3]	Evaluation; Homework; Further Study	Special Consideration / Accommodation
Mon.					
Tues.					
Wed.					
Thurs.					
Fri.					

[1] **Objective:** Given relative instructions, the student will be able to (TSWBAT)…
[2] **Procedure:** Using a variety of teaching strategies, learning styles and with relative supplementary materials, the teacher will…
[3] **Student Activity:** Having received instructions, and or with guided instructions, the student will…

Lesson Plan Template #2

ASSESS PRIOR TEACHER PREPARATION

OBJECTIVES:

RATIONALE:

STANDARD:

MATERIALS:

PROCEDURES/SETTING STAGE FOR STUDENT SUCCESS

DIFFERENTIATED INSTRUCTION

SPECIAL CONSIDERATIONS FOR EARLY FINISHERS

STUDENTS WITH SPECIAL NEEDS

LEARNING STYLES

HOMOGENOUS GROUPING

REMEDIATION:

ENRICHMENT:

SPECIAL ACCOMMODATIONS

Lesson Plan #3

SHORT STORY ANALYSIS

Name _____

Subject _____

Hour _____

Date _____

Objective: The student will demonstrate an understanding of the story by responding to the following:

Setting: Where does the story take place? _____

_____

_____

_____

_____

Characterization: Provide a brief description of the main characters.

_____

_____

_____

_____

_____

_____

_____

_____

_____

Conflict: What is the story's conflict, goal, or problem? _____

_____

_____

_____

_____

_____

Sequence: List the sequence of events in the story. _____

_____

_____

_____

_____

_____

Resolution: How did the story end? What was resolved? Were the goals reached, the problem solved, the conflict resolved? _____

_____

_____

_____

_____

_____

New Vocabulary learned:_____

_____

_____

_____

_____

_____

Emotional Intelligence lesson learned: _____

_____

_____

_____

_____

_____

Reflections: What stood out in your mind most and why? How can you apply lessons learned to your everyday life? _____

_____

_____

_____

_____

_____

Character Analysis: Venn Diagram

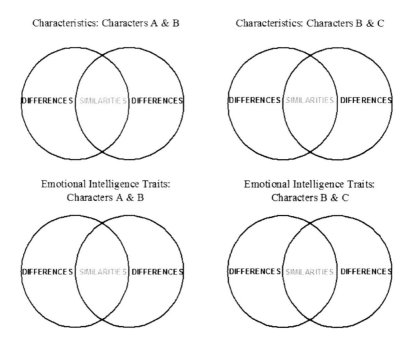

Characteristics: Characters A & B

DIFFERENCES SIMILARITIES DIFFERENCES

Characteristics: Characters B & C

DIFFERENCES SIMILARITIES DIFFERENCES

Emotional Intelligence Traits:
Characters A & B

DIFFERENCES SIMILARITIES DIFFERENCES

Emotional Intelligence Traits:
Characters B & C

DIFFERENCES SIMILARITIES DIFFERENCES

Venn diagrams can be created for every pair of characters in a story or novel. You can see how they can be tailored to compare EI traits. Remember to identify the emotional competencies you wish for them to include.

Reference List

Abi Samura, N. (2000). *The relationship between emotional intelligence and academic achievement in eleventh graders*. Retrieved May 17, 2005, from http://members.fortunecity. com/nadabs/research-intell2.html

Abraham, R. (1999). Emotional intelligence in organizations: A conceptualization. *Genetic, Social & General Psychology Monographs*, 125(2), 209-224.

Abrams, J. C. (1986). On learning disabilities: Affective considerations. *Journal of Reading, Writing, and Learning Disabilities*, 2, 189-196.

Alford, S. (2003). Science and Success: Sex Education and other Programs that work to prevent teen pregnancy, HIV, & sexually transmitted infections. Washington, DC: Advocates for Youth.

Allen, R. (2000). *Learning disabilities: At the assessment of crossroads*. Retrieved June 6, 2004, from http://www.ascd.org/ publications/curr_update/2000fall/allen.html

Alley, G. A., & Deshler, D. D. (1979). Teaching the learning-disabled adolescent: Strategies and methods. Denver, CO: Love.

Bachara, G. (1977). Empathy in learning-disabled children (F. McGlannan, Ed.). *Journal of Learning Disabilities, 10*(8), 42-43. (Reprinted from *Perceptual and Motor Skills*, 43, 541-542)

Bandura, A. (1969). *Principles of behavior modification*. New York: Holt, Reinhard, and Winston.

Bandura, A. (1973). *Aggression: A social learning analysis.* Englewood Cliffs, NJ: Prentice-Hall.

Bandura, A. (1977). *Social learning theory*. Englewood Cliffs, NJ: Prentice Hall.

Bar-On, R. (1988). *The development of a concept of psychological well-being.* Unpublished doctoral dissertation, Rhodes University, South Africa.

Bar-On, R. (1997). The Emotional Quotient Inventory (EQ-i): A Test of Emotional Intelligence. Toronto: Multi-Health Systems.

Bar-On, R. (2000). Emotional and social intelligence: Insights from the Emotional Quotient Inventory. In R. Bar-On & J. D. A. Parker (Eds.), *The handbook of emotional intelligence* (pp. 343-362). San Francisco: Jossey-Bass.

Bar-On, R. (2005). The Bar-On model of emotional-social intelligence (Special Issue on emotional intelligence, P. Fernandez-Berrocal & N. Extremera, Guest Eds.). *Psicothema*, 17, 1-28.

Bar-On, R., & Parker, J. D. (2000). The handbook of emotional intelligence: Theory, development, assessment, and application at home, school, and in the workplace. San Francisco: Jossey-Bass.

Barton, K., Dielman, T. E., & Cattell, R. B. (1972). Personality and IQ measures as predictors of school achievement. *Journal of Educational Psychology*, 63(4) 398-404.

Baumel, J. (2003). Learning disabilities: An overview: A parent's guide to helping kids with learning disabilities. Retrieved August 4, 2005, from www.Schwablearning .org

Berger, K. S. (1994). *The developing person through the life span* (3rd ed.). New York: Worth.

Bergert, S. (2000). *Warning signs of learning disabilities*. Eric EC Digest. Retrieved August 12, 2004, from http://ericec.org/ digests/e603.html

Bernet, M. (1996). Emotional intelligence: Components and correlates. *Journal of Learning Disabilities*, 34, 66-85. (ERIC Document Reproduction Service No. ED408535)

Binet, A. (2004). *What does "IQ" stand for and what does it mean?* Retrieved August 8, 2004, from http://www.geocities.com. rnseitz/Definition_of_IQ.html

Bluman, A. (1998). *Elementary statistics: A step by step approach* (3rd ed.). Boston: McGraw-Hill.

Boudah, D., & Weiss, M. (2002). *Learning disabilities overview*. Retrieved August 23, 2005, from http://eric.org/digests/e624.html

Brigance, A. (1999). *Brigance comprehensive inventory of basic skills– revised*. North Billerica, MA: Curriculum Associates.

Broder, P. K., Dunviant, N., Smith, E. E. C., & Sutton, L. P. (1981). Further observations on the link between learning disabilities and juvenile delinquency. *Journal of Educational Psychology*, 73, 838-850.

Brooks, G., Brooks, J. (1993). Assessments in a constructivist classroom. Retrieved February, 26, 2007 from http:www.ncrek.irg/sdrs/areas/issues/methods/assment/as7const.htm.

Bryant, D. P., Vaugh, S., Lina-Thompson, S., Ugel, N., & Hamff, A. (2000). Reading outcomes for students with and without learning disabilities in general-education middle-school content-area classes. *Learning Disability Quarterly*, 23(3), 24-38.

Bursuck, W. (1989). A comparison of students with learning disabilities to low-achieving and higher-achieving students on three dimensions of social competence. *Journal of Learning Disabilities, 22*, 188-194.

Carson, J., & Johnson, B. (1997). Attempting environmental education reform: Initiation and implementation of programmatic, outdoors environmental learning in public-school curricula. Retrieved August 8, 2004, from http://www.labtrobe.edu.auloent/ C_D_conference_2004

CASEL. (2004). *The collaborative for academic, social and emotional learning*. Retrieved August 15, 2004, from http://www.casel.org/ about_casel/history.php

Cattell, R. B., & Butcher, H. J. (1968). *The prediction of achievement and creativity*. New York: Irvington.

Ceci, S. J. (1994). Bioecological theory of intellectual development. In R. J. Sternberg (ed). *Encyclopedia of human intelligence* (pp. 568-587). New York: Macmillan.

Cherniss, C. (2000, April). *Emotional intelligence: What it is and why it matters*. Paper presented at the annual meeting of Society for Industrial and Organizational Psychology, New Orleans, LA.

Cook, G. (1989). Discourse in language teaching: A scheme for teacher education. Oxford: Oxford University Press.

Cronk, B. C. (1999). *How to use SPSS: A step by step guide to analysis and interpretation*. Los Angeles: Pyrczak.

Deshler, D. D. (2005). Adolescents with learning disabilities: Unique challenges and reasons for hope. *Journal of Learning Disability Quarterly*, 28, 122-124.

Dudley-Marling, C. (2004). The social construction of learning disabilities. *Learning Disabilities*, 37(6), 482-489.

Dyson, L. L. (2003). Children with learning disabilities within the family context: A comparison with siblings in global self-concept, academic self-perception, and social competence. *Learning Disabilities Research & Practice*, 18 (1), 1-9.

Edelman, M. W. (1996). In the forward to L. Lantieri & J. Patti, *Waging peace in our schools*. Boston: Beacon Press.

Edutopia. (2001). *Daniel Goleman on emotional intelligence*. Retrieved April 17, 2005, from http://www.edutopia.org/php/interview.php?id=Art_699&key=020

Edutopia. (2004). *Daniel Goleman: Developmental-studies center child-development program*. Retrieved August 11, 2004, from http://www/glef.org/php/orgs .php?id=ORG_301661

Ekman, P. (1992). An argument for basic emotions. *Cognition and Emotion*, 6, 169-200.

Elder, L. (1997). Critical thinking: The key to emotional intelligence. *Journal of Developmental Education,* 21(1), 40-41.

Elias, M. J. (2004). The connection between social/emotional learning and learning disabilities: Implications for intervention, *Disabilities Quarterly,* 27, 53-59.

Elias, M. J., Gara, M., Schuyler, T., Brandon-Muller, L. R., & Sayette, M. A. (1991). The promotion of social competence: Longitudinal study of a preventive school-based program. *American Journal of Orthopsychiatry,* 61(3), 409-417.

Elias, M. J., & Weissberg, R. P. (2000). Primary prevention: Educational approaches to enhance social and emotional learning. *Journal of School Health,* 70(5), 186-188.

Elias, M. J., Zins, J. E., Weissberg, R. P., Frey, K. S., Greenberg, M. T., Haynes, N. M., et al. (1997). *Promoting social and emotional learning: Guide-lines for educators*. Alexandria, VA: ASCD.

Elksnin, L., & Elksnin, N. (1995). *Assessment and instruction of social skills*. San Diego: Singular.

Elksnin, L., & Elksnin, N. (1998). Teaching social skills to students with language and behavior problems. *Intervention in School & Clinic*, 33, 131-140.

Elksnin, L., & Elksnin, N. (2001). Adolescents with disabilities: The need for occupational skills training. *Exceptionality,* 9(1 & 2), 91-100.

Elksnin, L., & Elksnin, N. (2005). Fostering social-emotional learning in the classroom. *Journal of Education*, 124(1), 74.

EQ Today. (2000). *Emotional what? Definitions and history of emotional intelligence.* Retrieved August 10, 2004, from http://www.eqtoday.com/02/emotional.php

Erikson, E. H. (1950). *Childhood and society.* New York: Norton.

Erikson, E. H. (1959). *Identity and the life cycle.* New York: Norton.

Erikson, E. H. (1963). *Childhood and society* (2nd ed.). New York: Norton.

Erikson, E. H. (1980). On the generational cycle: An address. *International Journal of Psychoanalysis, 61,* 213-224.

Farmer, T. W. (2000). Misconceptions of peer rejection and problem behavior: Understanding aggression in students with mild disabilities. *Remedial and Special Education, 21,* 194-208.

Finland, T. G. (2004). *The imaginary disease.* Westport, CT: Bergin & Garvey.

Frengut, R. (2004). *Social acceptance of students with learning disabilities.* Retrieved August 9, 2005, from http://www.Idanatl.org/aboutld/teachers/social_emotional/print_social acceptance.asp

Friend, M. (2006). IDEA 2004: Special-education contemporary perspectives for school professionals (Updated ed.). Boston: Pearson Education.

Fuchs, L. S., & Fuchs, D. (1998). Building a bridge across the canyon. *Learning Disability Quarterly*, 21, 99-101.

Fullan, M. (1991). *The new meaning of educational change* (2nd ed.). New York: Teachers College Press.

Fullan, M. (1993). Change forces: Probing the depths of educational reform. New York: Falmer Press.

Fullan, M. (2001). *Leading in a culture of change*. San Francisco: Jossey-Bass.

Fullan, M., & Miles. M. (1992, June). Getting reform right: What works and what doesn't. *Phi Delta Kappan*, 745-752.

Gardner, H. (1983). Frames of mind: The theory of multiple intelligences. New York: Basic Books.

Gardner, H. (1986). The waning of intelligence tests. In R. J. Sternberg & D. Dettrman (Eds.), *What is intelligence?* (pp. 73-76). Hillsdale, NJ: Erlbaum.

Gardner, H. (1995, Winter). Cracking open the IQ box. *The American Prospect, 20*, 71.

Garrett, D. (1995, Spring). Violent behaviors among African-American adolescents. *Adolescence*, 30(117), 209-215.

Gaskins, I. W. (1984). There's more to a reading problem than poor reading. *Journal of Learning Disabilities*, 17(8), 467-470.

Gerson-Wolfensberger, D. C. M., & Ruijssenaars, W. A. (1997). Definition and treatment of dyslexia: A report by the Committee on Dyslexia of the Health Council of the Netherlands. *Journal of Learning Disabilities*, 30, 209-213.

Gersten, R., Fuchs, L. S., Williams, J. P., & Baker, S. (2001). Teaching reading comprehension strategies to students with learning disabilities. *Review of Educational Research*, 71, 279-320.

Goleman, D. (1995*). Emotional intelligence*. New York: Bantam Books.

Goleman, D. (1998a, November/December). What makes a leader? *Harvard Business Review*, 76, 93-102.

Goleman, D. (1998b). *Working with emotional intelligence*. New York: Bantam.

Goleman, D. (2001). Emotional intelligence: Issues in paradigm building. In C. Cherniss & D. Goleman (Eds.), *The emotionally intelligent workplace* (pp. 13-36). San Francisco: Jossey-Bass.

Good, T. L., & Brophy, J. E. (1998). *Helping students construct knowledge: Looking in classrooms*. Ontario, Canada: Addison Wesley Longman.

Gorman, J. C. (1999). Understanding children's hearts and minds: Emotional functioning and learning disabilities. *Journal of Teaching Exceptional Children*, 31(3), 71-77.

Graczyk, P., Weissberg, J., Payton, J., Elias, M., Greenberg, M., & Zins, J. (2000). Criteria for evaluating the quality of school-based social and emotional learning programs. In *The handbook of emotional intelligence: Theory, development, assessment, and application at home, school, and in the workplace* (pp. 391-407). San Francisco: Jossey-Bass.

Graczyk, R., Weissberg, R. P., & Payton, J. P. (2000). Criteria for evaluating the quality of school-based social and emotional learning programs. In R. P. Bar-On, & J. D. A. Parker (Eds.), *Handbook of emotional intelligence: Theory, development, assessment, and application at home, school and in the workplace* (pp. 391-410). San Francisco: Jossey-Bass.

Gray, J. (1993). *Men are from Mars and women are from Venus.* New York: Harper Collins.

Greenham, S. L. (1999). Learning disabilities and psychosocial adjustment: A critical review. *Child Neuropsychology*, 5, 171-196.

Greenleaf, R. K. (2003a, May 3). Motion and emotion. *Principal Leadership*, 9, 14-19.

Greenleaf, R. K. (2003b). Motion and emotion in student learning. *Education Digest*, 69 (1), 38.

Gregory, R. J. (2000). Psychological testing: History, principles, and applications (3rd ed.). Boston: Allyn and Bacon.

Gresham, F. M. (1992). Social skills and learning disabilities: Causal, concomitant, or correlational? *Journal of School Psychology Review*, 21(3), 348.

Grolick, W. S., & Ryan, R. M. (1990). Self-perceptions, motivations, and adjustment in children with learning disabilities: A multiple-group comparison study. *Journal of Learning Disabilities*, 23, 177-184.

Hallahan, D. P. (2000). *William M. Cruickshank: If he were alive today.* International Dyslexia Association Conference, Washington, DC.

Hallahan, D. P., & Kaufman, J. M. (1976). *Introduction to learning disabilities: A psycho-behavioral approach.* Englewood Cliffs, NJ: Prentice-Hall.

Hallahan, D. P., & Kauffman, J. (1997). *Exceptional learners* (7th ed.). Boston: Allyn & Bacon.

Handwerk, M., & Marshall, R. M. (1998). Behavioral and emotional problems of students with learning disabilities, serious emotional disturbance, or both conditions. *Journal of Learning Disabilities*, 31, 327-338.

Harrington-Lueker, D. (1997). Students need emotional intelligence. *Educational Digest*, 63(1), 7.

Harrod, N. R., & Scheer, S. D. (2005). An exploration of adolescent emotional intelligence in relation to demographic characteristics. *Adolescence*, 40(59), 503.

Hein, S. (2004). *History and definition of emotional intelligence*. Retrieved July 14, 2004, from http://equi.org/history.htm

Hinshelwood, J. (1907). Four cases of congenital word-blindness occurring in the same family, *British Medical Journal*, 2, 1229-1232. Cited in History of Learning Disabilities. Retrieved September 28, 2004, from http://ac.marywood.edu/ maglioli/wwhistory.htm

Hinshelwood, J. (1917). *Congenital word blindness*. London: Lewis.

Holder, H. B., & Kirkpatrick, S. (1991). Interpretation of emotion from facial expressions in children with and without learning disabilities. *Journal of Learning Disabilities*, 24(3), 170.

Individual Disabilities Education Act (IDEA), 34 C.F.R. § 300.7 (c) 10 (2004).

Isen, A. M. (1984). Toward understanding the role of affect in cognition. In R. S. Wyler & T. K. Srull (Eds.), *The handbook of social cognition: Vol. 3* (pp. 179-236). Hillsdale, NJ: Erlbaum.

Isom, M. D. (1998). *The social learning theory*. Retrieved January 3, 2005, from http://www.criminology.fsu.edu/crimtheory/bandura.htm

Jacobs, T. O., & Jacquies, E. (1990). Military executive leadership. In K. E. Clark & M. B. Clark (Eds.), *Measures of leadership* (p. 281). West Orange, NJ: Leadership of America.

Jenkins, J., Barksdale, A., & Clinton, L. (1978). Improving reading comprehension and oral reading: Generalization across behaviors, settings, and time. *International Journal of Disability*, 11(10), 607-611.

Jenkins, S., Buboltz, W., Jr., Schwartz, J., & Johnson, P. (2005). Differentiation of self and psychosocial development. *Contemporary Family Therapy*, 27(2), 251-255.

Johnson, R. T., Johnson, D. W. (1986). Action research: *Cooperative learning in the science classroom*. Science and Children, 24, 31-32.

Karlsen, B., & Gardner, E. (1955). *Stanford Diagnostic Reading Test* (4th ed.) Orlando, FL: Harcourt Educational Measurement.

Katyal, S., & Awasthi, E. (2005). Gender differences in emotional intelligence among adolescents of Chandigarh. *Journal of Human Ecology*, 17(2), 153.

Kavale, K. A., & Forness, S. R. (1996). Social skills deficits and learning disabilities: A meta-analysis. *Journal of Learning Disabilities*, 29, 226-237.

Kirk, S. A., McCarthy, J. J., & Kirk, W. D. (1968). *Illinois Test of Psycholinguistic Abilities* (Rev. ed.). Urbana, IL: University of Illinois Press.

Kirsch, L., Jungeblut, A., Jenkins, L., & Kolstad, A. (1993). *Adult literacy in America*. Washington, DC: Educational Testing Service.

Kusche, C. A., & Greenberg, M. T. (1994). *Teaching PATHS in your classroom: The PATHS curriculum instructional manual*. Seattle, WA: Developmental Research & Programs.

Lantieri, L. & Patti, J. (1999). *Waging peace in our schools*. Boston: Beacon Press.

Lawson, C. (2002). *The connections between emotions and learning*. Retrieved July 23, 2005, from http://www.cdl.org/resource-library/articles/connect_emotions.php

Leeper, R. W. (1948). A motivational theory of emotions to replace "emotions as a disorganized response." *Psychological Review*, 55, 5-21.

Lenz, B. K., & Hughs, C. A. (1990). A word identification strategy for adolescents with learning disabilities. *Journal of Learning Disabilities,* 23(3), 149-158.

Lerner, J. (1976). *Children with learning disabilities.* Boston: Houghton Mifflin.

Lerner, J. (2003). Learning disabilities: Theories, diagnoses, and teaching strategies (9th ed.). Boston: Houghton Mifflin.

Licknoma, T. (1991). Educating for character: How our schools can teach respect and responsibility. New York: Bantam.

Licht, B. G., & Kistner, J. A. (1986). Motivational problems of learning disabled children: Individual differences and their implications for treatment. In J. K. Torgenson & B. W. L. Wong (Eds.), *Psychological and educational perspectives on learning disabilities* (pp. 140-153). Orlando, FL: Academic Press.

Lynn, A. (2002). *The emotional intelligence activity book: 50 activities for promoting WQ at work.* New York: American Management Association.

Lyon, R. G. (1996). The future of children. Special Education for Students with Disabilities, 6, 1.

Lyon, R. G., & Fletcher, J. M. (2001). *Early warning system.* Retrieved August 23, 2005, from http://www.educationnext. org/20012/22.html

Mann, L., Goodman, L., & Wiederholt, J. L. (1978). *Teaching the learning disabled adolescent.* Boston: Houghton Mifflin.

Mastropieri, M. A., & Scruggs, T. (1997). Best practices in promoting reading comprehension in students with learning disabilities. *Remedial & Special Education, 18*(4), 197.

Mather, N., & Gregg, N. (2006, Spring). Specific learning disabilities: Clarifying, not eliminating a construct. *Journal of Psychoeducation Assessment, 24*, 75-84.

Mayer, J. D., & Salovey, P. (1997). What is emotional intelligence? Emotional development and emotional intelligence: Implications for educators. New York: Basic Books.

McClung, A.C. (2000). Extramusical skills in the music classroom. *Music Educatars Journal*, 86(5), 32-34.

McCluskey, A. (2000). *Emotional intelligence in schools*. Retrieved January 17, 2005, from http://www.connected.org/ learn/school.html

McPhail, J. (1993). Adolescents with learning disabilities: A comparative life-stream interpretation. *Journal of Learning Disabilities*, 26(9), 617-620.

Mergel, B. (1998). *Instructional design & learning theory*. Retrieved April 11, 2005, from http://www.usak.ca/education/coursework/ 802papers/mergel/brenda.htm

Office of Special Education. (2000). *What is a learning disability? U. S. Federal Code (Section 300. 7 c (10) of 34 CFR 300 and 303)*. Retrieved August 5, 2004, from http://curry.edschool.virginia.edu/ sped/projects/ose/categories/Id.html

Ormsbee, C. K. (2000). [Review of the book Developing emotional intelligence]. *Journal of Intervention in School and Clinic*, 36(2), 125-126.

Pathways to the 21st century learning: High school English curriculum guide: Transformation, reflection and vision. (2001). Detroit, MI: Detroit Public Schools.

Payne, W. L. (1986). A study of emotion: Developing emotional intelligence; self-integration; relating to fear, pain and desire. *Dissertation Abstracts International, 47*(1-A), 203A. (UMI No. AAD9-5947)

Pediatric Behavioral Health Resources, LLC. (2003). Retrieved August 9, 2005, from http://www.earlychildhoodbehavioralhealth. com/Print/CDSocSkills.htm

Pellitter, J. (2006). Emotional intelligent interventions for students with reading disabilities. *Reading & Writing Quarterly*, 22, 155-171.

Phillips, D. C., & Soltis, F. (1998). *Perspective on learning.* New York: Teachers College Press.

Pickar, D. B., & Tori, C. D. (1986). The learning disabled adolescent: Eriksonian psychosocial development, self-concept, and delinquent behavior. *Journal of Youth and Adolescence*, 15(5), 429-440.

Pinter, R. (1921). Intelligence. In E. L. Thorndike (ed.), Intelligence and its measurement: A symposium. *Journal of Educational Psychology*, 12, 123-147.

Rauch, C. F., & Behling, D. (1984). Functionalism: Basis for an alternate approach to the study of leadership. In J. G. Hunt, D. M. Hosking, C. A. Schriesheim, & R. Stewart (Eds.), *Leaders and managers: International perspectives on managerial behavior and leadership* (p. 46). Elmsford, NY: Pergamon Press.

Reiff, H., Hatzes, N., Bramel, M. H., & Gibbon, T. (2001). The relation of LD and gender with emotional intelligence in college students. *Journal of Learning Disabilities*, 34(1), 66-78.

Resnick, M., Bearman, P. S., Blum, R. W., Bauman, K. E., Harris, K. M., Hones, J., et al. (1997). Protecting adolescents from harm. *Journal of the American Medical Association*, 278, 823-832.

Richards, D., & Engle, S. (1986). After the vision: Suggestions to corporate visionaries and vision champions. In J. D. Adams (Ed.), *Transforming leadership* (pp. 199-215). Alexandria, VA: Miles River Press.

Richburg, M., & Fletcher, T. (2002). Emotional intelligence: Directing a child's emotional education. *Journal of Child Study*, 32(1), 31-33.

Rust, F. O., & Freidus, H. (Eds.). (2001). *Guiding school change: The role and work of change agents*. New York: Teachers College Press.

Salovey, P., & Mayer, J. (1990). Emotional intelligence, imagination and cognition, and personality. *Educational Psychologist*, 9, 185-211.

Salovey, P., & Sluyter, D. (1997). *Emotional development and emotional intelligence*. New York: Basic Books.

Schaps, E., Battistich,V., & Solomon, D. (1997). School as a caring community: A key to character education. In A. Molnar (Ed.), *The construction of children's character, Part II: 96th yearbook of the National Society for the Study of Education.* Chicago: University of Chicago Press.

Schein, E. H. (1992). *Organizational culture and leadership* (2nd ed.). San Francisco: Jossey-Bass.

Schunk, D. (2000). *Learning theories an educational perspective* (3rd ed.). Upper Saddle River, NJ: Prentice-Hall, Pearson Education.

Schwab-Stone, M. (2004). *CASEL: The Collaborative for the Advancement of Social and Emotional Learning.* Retrieved August 15, 2004, from http://www.nmha.org/ prevention/update/case.html

Shapiro, L. E. (1998). *How to raise a child with a high EQ: A parent's guide to emotional intelligence*. New York: Harper Collins.

Siegel, L. S. (1996). Learning disabilities: The roads we have traveled and the path to the future. In R. J. Sternberg & L. Spear-Swerling (Eds.), *Perspectives on learning disabilities: Biological, cognitive, contextual* (pp. 159-161). Boulder, CO: West View Press.

Six ways to build character in the classroom. (2001, February). *Curriculum Review*, 40(6), 6.

Stanovich, K. E. (2000). *Progress in understanding reading: Scientific foundations and new frontiers*. New York: Guilford Press.

Stock, Byron, and Associates. (1999). *Emotional intelligence (EI)*. Retrieved July 4, 2004, from http://www.byronstock.com/ whatisei1234.html

Stone-McCowan, K. (1993, November 7). *The New York Times*.

Strydom, J., & du Plessis. S. (2000). *The right to read. Diagnosis learning disabilities*. Retrieved August 9, 2004, from http://www/audioblox2000.com/book4.htm

Strydom, J., & du Pless, S. (2002). The right to read: Beating dyslexia and other learning disabilities. Retrieved August 4, 2004, from http://www.audioblox2000.com/ book6.htm

Strydom, J., & du Plessis, S. (2004). *The right to read: Definitions on the web*. Retrieved August 9, 2004, from http://www/audioblox2000.com/book4.htm

Sutarso, T., Baggert, L. K., Sutarso, P., & Tapia, M. (1996). *Effect of gender and GPA on emotional intelligence.* Paper presented at the annual meeting of the Mid-South Educational Research Association, Tuscaloosa, AL.

Thorndike, E. L. (1920). Intelligence and its uses. *Harper's Magazine*, 140, 227-235.

Torgesen, J. K. (2000). Individual differences in response to early interventions in reading: The lingering problem of treatment resisters. *Learning Disabilities Research & Practice*, 15, 55-64.

U. S. Department of Education. (2000). Twenty-second annual report to Congress on the implementation of the Individuals with Disabilities Act. Washington, DC: Author.

Valencia Faculty, Four Channels of Learning Retrieved 2001 from http://faculty.valencia.cc.fl.us/ffarquharson/FourMajChan.html.

Van Etten, G., & Van Etten, C, (1976). The measurement of pupil progress and selecting Instructional materials. *Journal of Learning Disabilities, 2*(8), 4-19.

Vygotsy, L.S. (1978). Mind in society. The development of higher psychological processes. Cambridge, MA:MIT Press,

Vaughn, S., Bos, C. S., & Schumm, J. S. (2006). IDEA 2004: Teaching exceptional, diverse, and at-risk students in the general education classroom (Updated ed.). Boston: Pearson Education.

Wallace, G., Larson, S. C., & Elksnin, L. D. (1992). *Educational assessment of learning problems: Testing for teaching.* Boston: Allyn and Bacon.

Webster's new dictionary and thesaurus. (2002). Cleveland, OH: Wiley.

World Book Dictionary. (1979). Chicago: Doubleday.

Weissberg, R. P., Caplan, M. Z., & Sivo, P. J. (1989). A new conceptual framework for establishing school-based social competence promotion programs. In L. A. Bond & B. E. Compas (Eds.), *Primary prevention and promotion in the schools* (pp. 255-296). Newbury Park, CA: Sage.

Weissinger, H. (1998). *Emotional intelligence at work.* San Francisco: Jossey-Bass.

Wolf, M., & Katzir-Cohen, T. (2001). Reading fluency and its intervention (Special issue on fluency, E. Kameenui & D. Simmons, Eds.). *Scientific Studies Reading*, 5, 211-218.

Wong, B. Y. L. (1996). *The ABCs of learning disabilities.* San Diego, CA: Academic Press.

Yukl, G. (1998). *Leadership in organizations* (4th ed.). Upper Saddle River, NJ: Prentice Hall.

Zambo, D., & Brem, S. (2004). Emotion and cognition in students who struggle to read: New insights and ideas. *Reading Psychology*, 25, 189-204.

Zeidner, M., Richard, R., & Matthews, G. (2002). Can emotional intelligence be schooled? A critical review. *Educational Psychology*, 37(4), p. 229.

Zenger, J. H. (1970, July). A comparison of human development with psychological development in T. groups. *Training and Development Journal*, 16-20.

Zirker, S. (2000). Social intelligence: The development and maintenance or purposive behavior. In R. Bar-On & J. D. A. Parker (Eds.), *The handbook of intelligence: Theory, development, assessment, and application at home, school, and in the workplace* (p. 5). San Francisco: Jossey-Bass.

About the Author

Helen C. Bryant, PhD, President and Founder of Life Learning Essentials, LLC, possesses over thirty years of experience as president of various non-profit organizations and as a former public high school teacher. Dr. Bryant uses her background and professional experience to facilitate  leadership workshops, deliver expert keynote addresses, and provide emotional-intelligence and team-building training sessions, as well as current cutting-edge presentations. As an educator, she offers instructional strategies for creating an emotionally intelligent classroom for students with or without learning disabilities. Dr. Bryant helps leaders, individuals, teachers, churches, and organizations build effective teams. As an experienced leader and teacher, her desire is to empower, current and future leaders with practical and effective life-learning essentials.

Dr. Bryant holds a Bachelor's and Master's Degree from Wayne State University, and a PhD in Leadership from Andrews University. Her dissertation research topic was "The Relationship Between Emotional

Intelligence and Reading Comprehension in High School Students with Learning Disabilities." She holds a Professional Education Teaching Certificate in Social Science, Cognitive Impairment, Physical and Otherwise Health Impairments, Teacher of the Homebound, and Learning Disabilities. During her tenure as an educator, she has held positions as a classroom and resource-room teacher, interim Department Head of Specialized Student Services, and Teacher Consultant for students with special needs. She is certified in using EQi and EQ 360 Assessments.

Dr. Bryant's leadership, presentations, and expertise stretch internationally. She has conducted workshops for teachers and taught at the Maxwell Preparatory Academy in Nairobi, Kenya, as an Operation Reach Back Volunteer. Dr. Bryant has been the recipient of Numerous Leadership Awards and has been listed multiple times in "Who's Who Among America's Teachers. She is a mentor, presenter, speaker and Emotional Intelligence Coach. Dr. Bryant is the proud parent of two daughters (Sharona Bryant, MD, Venitress Carrington, DDS) and a teenage son (Kyle Miller).

Available Now:

The Relationship between Emotional Intelligence and
Reading Comprehension (Dissertation)

Serving and Learning to Lead with Emotional Intelligence

Upcoming Emotional Intelligence Symposium – 2012

For Further Details:

EQ-i Workshops/Consultations

Team Building

EI Coaching

EI Assessments

www.lifelearningessentials.com

Telephone/Fax 248-327-6755

CPSIA information can be obtained at www.ICGtesting.com
Printed in the USA
LVOW130115170911

246507LV00002B/2/P